READY
SET serge

READY SET serge

QUICK & EASY PROJECTS YOU CAN MAKE IN MINUTES

GEORGIE
MELOT

CINCINNATI, OHIO
www.MyCraftivity.com
Connect. Create. Explore.

fw
F+W PUBLICATIONS, INC.

Published by KP Craft Books, an imprint of F+W Publications, Inc., 4700 East Galbraith Road, Cincinnati, Ohio, 45236. (800) 289-0963. First Edition.

Other fine Krause Publications titles are available from your local bookstore, craft supply store, online retailer or visit our website at www.fwpublications.com.

12   11   10   09   08   5   4   3   2   1

Distributed in Canada by Fraser Direct
100 Armstrong Avenue
Georgetown, ON, Canada L7G 5S4
Tel: (905) 877-4411

Distributed in the U.K. and Europe by David & Charles
Brunel House, Newton Abbot, Devon, TQ12 4PU, England
Tel: (+44) 1626 323200, Fax: (+44) 1626 323319
Email: postmaster@davidandcharles.co.uk

Distributed in Australia by Capricorn Link
P.O. Box 704, S. Windsor NSW, 2756 Australia
Tel: (02) 4577-3555

Library of Congress Cataloging-in-Publication Data

Melot, Georgie, 1960-
  Ready, set, serge: quick & easy projects you can make in minutes /
Georgie Melot.— 1st ed.
      p. cm.
  Includes includes bibliographical references and index.
  ISBN-13: 978-0-89689-690-1 (pbk : alk. paper)
1. Serging. I. Title.
  TT713.M44 2009
  646.2'044—dc22 2008041082

Edited by Nancy Breen and Layne Vanover
Interior designed by Nicole Armstrong
Production coordinated by Matt Wagner
Cover designed by Jennifer Hoffman
Cover photographed by Al Parrish
Cover photo styled by Jan Nickum

About the Author

Georgie and her husband, Max, live in Yukon, Oklahoma, where they have raised their two sons, Matthew and Mitchell. Georgie, a full-time special education teacher who spends her free time pursuing her lifelong love of sewing, is proficient with the sewing machine and serger and in all aspects of machine embroidery. Georgie taught her first sewing class over 25 years ago and has taught throughout the United States. Her classes, patterns and curriculum make the learning process enjoyable and successful for all.

Metric Conversion Chart

To convert	to	multiply by
Inches	Centimeters	2.54
Centimeters	Inches	0.4
Feet	Centimeters	30.5
Centimeters	Feet	0.03
Yards	Meters	0.9
Meters	Yards	1.1

Acknowledgments

I want to thank all my family for their unquestionable belief in me. Max, Matthew and Mitchell: I also want to thank you for taking over when I spent long hours at the computer and the serger. Your joy in my accomplishments has been a blessing to me.

Becky, Gwen and Mary: A girl has never had better friends. You have gone above and beyond during this venture of mine. Thank you for your encouragement, the phone calls to keep me on schedule, proofing and testing my directions, letting me vent and, most importantly, for just being there. I could not have done this without you!

Deborah and Pam: Working for each of you has brought out the best of me. You are the model of what a boss should be. Your support, compassion and empathy make those you work with want to go the extra mile. Thank you for all you have taught me but mostly for being a friend.

Emily, Jan, Judy, Margaret, Missy, Rosalie, Susan and Teresa: You are such a talented group of women; and I am thankful for the time we were able to work together. I'll always remember the day we first met and I realized that there were others just like me! Your passion for sewing and your enthusiasm for what we do are an inspiration.

Jan: Thank you for dropping everything to take the pictures on such short notice. It was hard work, but I really enjoyed the time we spent together.

P & B Textiles: Thank you for providing the gorgeous fabric for all the projects in this book. Julie, you were great to work with and so helpful and prompt with all of our communications.

Dedication

For Matthew and Mitchell: Of all of God's blessings in my life, being your momma has been the best.

Table of Contents

Chapter 4

layering fabric

Chapter 5

serging into the curves

Chapter 6

remaking the ready-made

Introduction

Over the years I have taught many serger classes. It's always surprised me how many of my students owned sergers, sometimes for years, and yet were unable to use these wonderful machines. I decided that I needed to remedy that problem; but first I had to figure out why serger owners couldn't learn to use their sergers.

I sat myself down and tried to figure out how I learned to use my serger. I never took a class all those twenty-plus years ago; there was no such thing. I remember unpacking my serger and letting it sit on my sewing counter for about two weeks before I got up the nerve to thread it. Once I had that little machine threaded, I began serging—and I serged daily. I was doing alterations for three department stores at the time and hemmed 50–100 pairs of men's slacks weekly. I know you are probably questioning my sanity at this point, but doing alterations made it possible for me to be home with my boys. Besides, I had an industrial blind hemmer that allowed me to hem a pair of pants in a matter of minutes.

I serged the hems of all those slacks, and an amazing thing happened: I overcame any fears I had of the serger. (This was before I knew that I could do more with my serger than a 4-thread overlock).

That's when it came to me. Most serger classes and/or projects use several techniques and decorative stitches, so the students sitting behind the sergers are overwhelmed before the class or project has barely begun. Serger owners need to get comfortable with the serger *before* they are introduced to the specialty techniques and decorative stitches the serger is capable of.

So, you see, it's not your fault that you haven't mastered your serger. The problem lies in the way we educators have been teaching technique overload.

Once I knew what the problem was, I just needed to come up with the solution. Of course, everyone could serge the hem of 50–100 pairs of slacks each week, but that's not very much fun. So my mission was to create serger projects that used only a 4-thread overlock, thus eliminating technique overload.

With this book, I have accomplished my mission. You are on your way to serger success! There are sixteen serger projects in this book that you will have fun making with a 4-thread overlock stitch. The projects are quick enough that you can make several at a time and forgiving enough that your serging stitches don't have to be perfect. No stressing over these projects is allowed.

In no time at all you will overcome your serger fears and want to learn some of those specialty techniques and decorative stitches. Since the day will come when you are ready to move beyond the basic 4-thread overlock, this book has a *Stepped-Up* version of each of the sixteen projects. Each of these *Stepped-Up* projects will include a special technique or decorative stitch, allowing you to learn the new techniques one at a time, without technique overload.

I know you have the "urge to serge." The projects in this book are going to allow you to fulfill that urge. So, ready (get out your fabric), set (dust off your serger), now serge!

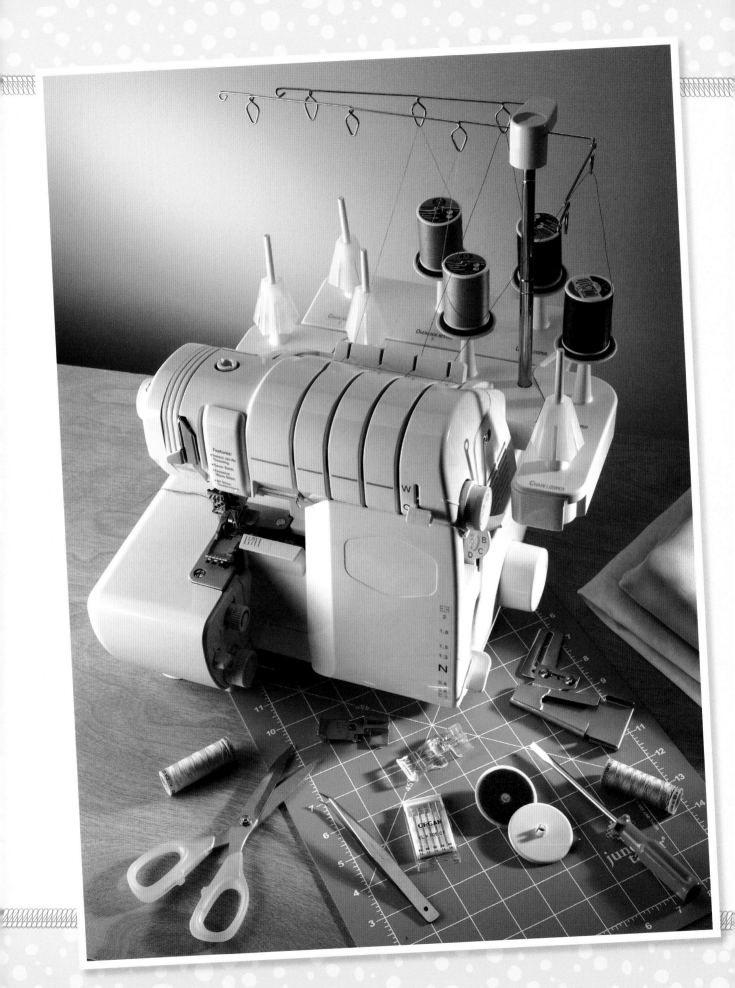

1

Getting to Know
Your Serger

Whether you've wanted to serge for years or for just a few days, you may be asking the same question: I have a serger—so what do I do now?

That's a good question. Whether you've heard scary serger stories or can share a few of your own, you may find your serger intimidating.

All you need is a tour of your serger with an expert guide to show you the way. Let me alleviate your fears as we explore this wonderful machine. We'll work our way through the threading maze, de-stress tension settings and marvel at those amazing features we don't find on our sewing machines.

Hope you're as excited to get started as I am.

Threading Your Serger

Threading is the first step in serging. Many consider it the most difficult step. That may be why many serger owners haven't mastered the serger.

Just as most sewing machines are threaded the same way, so are most sergers. The thread goes through a thread guide or two, then through the tension disks, then through another thread guide or two, and finally through the needles or loopers. It sounds easy enough, doesn't it? The problems arise from having to multiply the threading process three or four times.

When you're serging the basic overlock stitch, you use one or two needles and two loopers. It can get confusing when you're trying to determine which thread guide goes with which tension dial—or looper—or needle.

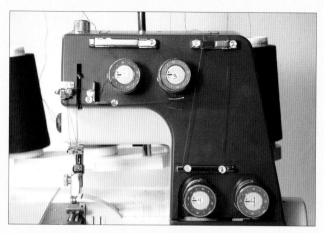

Numbers Written on Small Adhesive Dots
Different colors indicate each thread path.

Color-Coded Thread Paths

The manufacturers must be listening to serger owners; new serger models attempt to make threading less complicated. For example, many sergers have color-coded thread paths.

If your thread paths are not clearly marked, make things easier on yourself and mark them. Using permanent markers or adhesive dots in different colors is one way to do this.

Another complication is that some sergers require the loopers to be threaded first and in a specific order. It's important to check your machine's manual for instructions and charts specifically written for your model.

Correct Positioning

The final threading obstacle is determining the correct position for the needles and loopers.

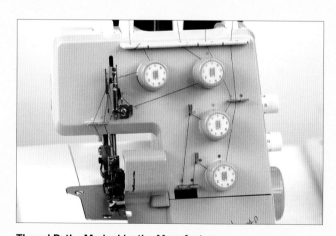

Thread Paths Marked by the Manufacturer
You may want to number them as well. Count as you thread to avoid missing a step.

Open the doors on your serger and roll the hand wheel. Notice how the loopers spread apart, then come back together and cross. When threading, it's important not to get the looper threads interlocked with each other. Again, check your manual for the correct needle/looper position when threading.

Manufacturer's marks on the hand wheel of one of my sergers indicate where the wheel should be positioned for threading. This makes the process much easier. If your hand wheel is not marked, determine the correct placement for threading and draw a line with a permanent marker.

Once you have determined your thread paths, threading order and appropriate needle/looper position, photocopy the chart below. Fill it in, including tension information, and keep it close by for easy reference. Better still, tape the chart to your serger until you become familiar with the threading process.

With One Stroke of a Marker
Drawing a simple line with a permanent marker eliminates the confusion of trying to remember where to position the needles and loopers.

Keep It Handy
You'll never have to search for your reference chart if you tape it to your machine.

THREADING CHART	Threading Order	Colored Path	# Steps for Threading	Threading Position
Lower Looper				
Upper Looper				
Left Needle				
Right Needle				
Tension Adjustments				

Needles and Loopers

While most sergers have two needles, some have only one. Still others have more than two. The needles stitch only a straight stitch, and there is no bobbin. The needle thread interlocks with the looper threads to create the stitches.

The serger has two loopers, an upper and a lower, for creating the basic overlock stitch. The upper looper is easier to thread. When it stitches, it moves above the fabric, so the upper looper thread lies on top of the fabric. The needle(s) slide into the upper thread loop before penetrating the fabric.

The lower looper is more difficult to thread. It moves below the fabric, so the lower looper thread lies on the bottom. The needle slides into the lower thread loop while penetrating the fabric. The looper threads do not penetrate the fabric; they encase the edge of the fabric.

If your serger is capable of creating a chain and/or cover stitch, it also has a chain looper. The chain looper moves below the fabric and interlocks with the needle thread. The chain looper thread lies on the bottom side of the fabric. The chain looper can be used for seaming or for decorative purposes.

At the back of the serger are spool pins to hold thread for the needles and loopers. The spool pins may be marked to indicate which thread goes on which pin. If your spool pins are not marked, I recommend labeling them—it will make the process easier as you learn to work with your serger.

Basic Overlock Stitch
The basic overlock stitch is created with two looper threads and two needle threads (left) or one needle thread (right).

Marked Spool Pins
Don't hesitate to write directly on your serger with a permanent marker. Correctly labeling your serger will save you much time and confusion.

Tension Settings

The tension settings on a serger work the same way they do on a sewing machine. When the presser foot is raised, there is no tension on the thread; when the presser foot is lowered, tension allows only the amount of thread needed for each stitch to pass through the tension disks. On a serger, each needle and looper thread has its own tension control system.

Adjusting Tension Settings

Most sergers allow adjustments so you can determine if the stitch requires more or less tension.

The easiest way to determine which tension control should be adjusted is to learn the placement of each of the threads within the stitch. When you're first playing with your serger, try threading each needle and looper with a different color of thread. That way, when you look at a serged seam, you can see the color of the thread that needs adjusting. In chapter two, we'll examine the anatomy of serger stitches to help you differentiate between the needle threads and the upper and lower looper threads.

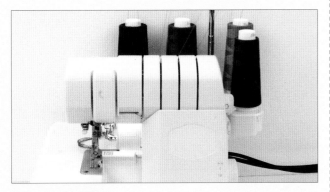

Follow the Colors
By using different colored threads for each needle and looper when you're practicing, you can learn to identify where each thread is placed within a stitch.

Make Accurate Adjustments

Once you've identified which tension control needs adjusting, you will need to determine how to manipulate the control accurately. If your serger has a knob, you can probably apply the old saying "righty-tighty, lefty-loosey" to tighten or loosen the tension.

If your serger has a tension dial or lever instead of a knob, it's probably marked with numbers or a plus (+) and minus (-) sign. Depending on your machine, turning the dial to a larger number (or the plus sign) could mean either of two things: 1) more tension or 2) more thread allowed to pass through the serger, which actually creates less tension.

Similarly, turning to a smaller number (or the minus sign) could mean either less tension or less thread allowed to pass through the serger (i.e., more tension). It's important to consult your serger manual to interpret the marks correctly on your tension controls.

Keep Track of Settings

Once you've figured out the tension controls on your serger, add the appropriate remarks to the threading chart (see page 13), such as "righty-tighty, lefty-loosey," "more tension, less tension" or "more thread, less thread."

Eventually you'll get to the point where you don't have to think about the tension adjustments. In the meantime, it will be easier if you don't have to look in the manual every time you need to adjust the tension.

SERGER HOW-TO: Doing a Tension Check

In the serging classes I've taught, when it comes to tension adjustments, the most common error I see is failing to raise the presser foot when threading the serger. If the presser foot is not raised, the threads cannot slide between the tension disks. Serging without any tension placed on the threads results in loopy stitches no amount of adjusting will fix.

To avoid this problem, I recommend that you do a quick tension check. Do the check on both needle threads and both looper threads.

1 Raise the presser foot. Pull each thread through the tension disk by grabbing the thread as it leaves the disk (it should pull through the disks easily).

Not Too Much Thread

Keep in mind that you don't want to pull massive amounts of thread through the tension disks. If the disks are plastic, continually pulling thread through them could wear grooves, requiring the disks to be replaced.

2 Lower the presser foot and test the pressure the tension disks have placed on the threads. You should be able to pull the threads through the tension disks but feel a gentle tightness. By gently pulling the thread as it leaves the tension disk, you will be able to closely adjust the tension before ever making a stitch.

Gauging "Gentle Tightness"

If you're not sure what *gentle tightness* feels like, do this same tension check with the needle thread on your sewing machine. This exercise will give you a good basis for gauging the correct tension on your serger threads.

3 If your tension is extremely tight or loose, make an adjustment.

4 When you feel that all the threads have a gentle tightness to the tension, make a sample stitch on the fabric you will be using.

5 Fine-tune the settings based on the stitch sample from Step 4.

First, look at the needle threads. They should be lying in a flat line on top of the fabric. You should see little-to-no needle threads on the underside of the fabric.

If the needle threads are creating small loops on the back or bottom side of the stitch, you need to tighten the tension.

If both needles appear to need adjusting, start with the left needle. When you have a good tension on the left needle, you may no longer need to adjust the right needle. If the right needle does need adjusting, make the changes at this point.

6 Next, check the looper threads. The upper looper threads should loop back and forth from the edge of the fabric to the needle threads and lie on top of the fabric. The lower looper thread also should loop back and forth from the edge of the fabric to the needle threads, but this thread lies on the bottom of the fabric as the stitches are made.

The looper threads interlock at the cut edge of the fabric. If one of the looper threads folds to the other looper side, the looper tensions need adjustment. The looper thread that does not go all the way to the edge will need to be loosened, while the looper thread that wraps to the wrong side will need to be tightened.

7 Continue to make stitch samples and tension adjustments until you have a well-balanced stitch. This means needle threads should lie flat on the top of the fabric with little-to-no thread showing on the underside, and the looper threads should loop from the needle threads to the edge of fabric.

Automatic Tension Settings

A few sergers have automatic tension regulation. I have found them to be very reliable in adjusting to different threads and fabrics. For most sergers, though, the tension settings will have to be adjusted manually.

Throat Plate and Cutting System

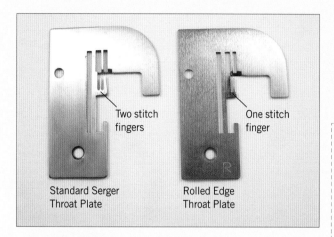

Two stitch fingers

One stitch finger

Standard Serger Throat Plate

Rolled Edge Throat Plate

There will be times, however, when you want to disengage the cutting system. Check your manual for the proper procedure for your machine. It may be as easy as flipping a switch, or you may have to take off a blade.

Throat Plate

The serger throat plate is similar to a sewing machine throat plate. The serger throat plate has stitch fingers, or little spikes that lie beside the needle area. The looper threads wrap around the stitch fingers as they encase the edges of the fabric. The stitch fingers keep the stitches flat.

Some sergers require you to change the throat plate to create a rolled edge. The rolled edge throat plate has less distance between the needle and the stitch finger, allowing the looper threads to pull or *roll* the edges of the fabric as it encases the fabric in the stitch.

There are sergers that allow you to move the needle area or cutting area, which eliminates the need to change throat plates for the rolled edge stitch.

The Cutting System

The serger is designed to trim off excess fabric as it serges. It has two blades, an upper and a lower blade, one or both of which move. Even if your project doesn't have excess fabric to trim away, you'll want to *trim hairs*, i.e., the loose threads along the cut edge of the fabric.

Cleaning

Like your sewing machine, your serger should be serviced regularly so it provices tip-top performance. In addition, perform your own regular maintenance by cleaning out the lint and thread that accumulate after each project. Most sergers come with a small brush for your machine. Use it often. I also find that canned air is great for cleaning my serger.

Differential Feed

My first serger did not have differential feed, and I don't know how I got along without it. The differential feed allows you to get perfect seams with fabrics that tend to pucker or stretch. You can create gathers or ease in fullness.

If your serger has differential feed, look for two sets of feed dogs: a front feed dog that controls the fabric as it goes under the foot, and a back feed dog that controls the fabric as it emerges.

How It Works

When the differential feed is set at 1.0 (or *normal*), the feed dogs work at the same rate. If you increase the differential feed, you increase the amount of fabric that is pushed under the foot compared to the rate the fabric is pushed out. If you reduce the differential feed, you reduce the amount of fabric pushed under the foot compared to the rate the fabric is pushed out.

So, what does that mean?

Another Explanation

Here's how it makes sense to me: Typically, the feed dogs work in conjunction with the needles, pushing a little fabric back and taking a stitch, pushing a little fabric back and taking a stitch. When you adjust the differential feed, the rate the fabric moves differs from the rate the needle penetrates the fabric.

If you increase the differential feed, you are moving more fabric through for each stitch; you will end up making small gathers or easing in fullness.

If you decrease the differential feed, you are moving less fabric through for each stitch. You will end up stretching the fabric.

Why would you want to stretch your fabric? If you're working with a fabric that tends to pucker, decreasing the differential feed will stretch out those puckers and give you a nice flat seam.

Creating Gathers
Increasing the differential feed allows you to create gathers as you finish the edge of the fabric.

Serger Feet

There are many serger feet available that do many different things. However, I've narrowed this discussion down to the feet that I find myself using the most.

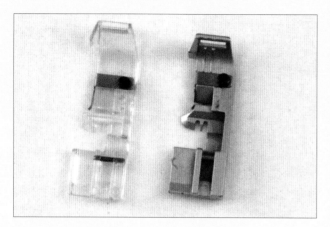

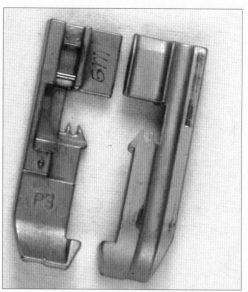

Standard Foot

This is the foot that comes with the serger and is used for most serging needs. Typically there are needle guide marks on the front of the foot.

A clear plastic foot is available for many machines. It allows you to see the fabric as it moves under the foot. This is useful for some of the specialty techniques and decorative stitches that you can create with your serger.

Cording Foot

With the cording (or piping) foot, you can create perfect piping with minimal effort.

The foot has a groove on the bottom that keeps your cording the ideal distance from the needles, creating perfect piping every time.

See the next page for a demonstration of how to use the cording foot.

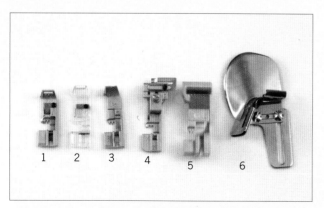

Those Fabulous Feet
1. Standard foot 2. Clear foot 3. Cording foot 4. Wire guide
5. Gathering foot 6. Double fold bias binder

SERGER HOW-TO: Using the Cording Foot

1 Cut a 2" (5cm) strip of fabric into the desired length. If your piping will be in curved areas, your strip should be cut on the bias.

2 Tuck the cording into the fabric strip, wrong sides together.

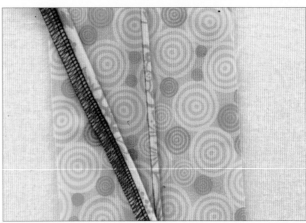

Perfect Piping
Never again will you have to settle for the solid-colored piping available in the fabric stores.

3 Place the cording and fabric under the foot, with the cording in the groove in the bottom of the foot. Serge to enclose the cording.

4 To attach, place the piping between the fabrics, right sides together, lining up the serged edge of the piping with the cut edges of the fabric. Serge into place.

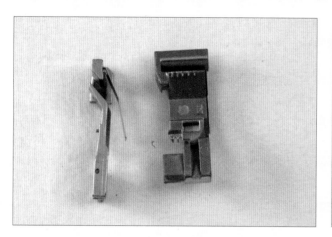

Gathering Foot

The gathering foot has an opening that guides fabric between the top portion of the foot and the bottom gathering plate. This allows you to gather one layer of fabric while attaching it to the fabric that will not be gathered.

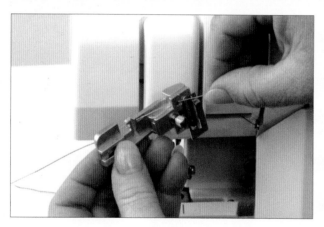

Wire Guide

The wire guide is not specifically a foot, but an attachment with holes through which a length of wire can be inserted. These holes line up the wire to the right of the needle, which allows the wire to be enclosed in a rolled edge. When the rolled edge is complete, the wire can be bent to shape the edge of the fabric.

Using the Gathering Foot
Put the fabric to be gathered next to the feed dog, right side up. Fabric not to be gathered is placed in the opening or mouth of the foot.

Beautifully Finished Ruffles
As the serger gathers one fabric and attaches it to another, it finishes the edges at the same time.

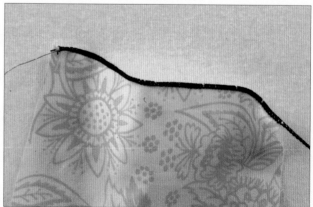

Shaping the Wire in the Rolled Edge

Double Fold Bias Binder

The double fold bias binder is an accessory used with the standard serger foot and the chain stitch to attach binding to the fabric edge.

The needle side of the binding looks like a straight row of stitching similar to that created on a sewing machine; the bottom or looper side of the binding shows a straight row of loops.

First, attach the binding accessory according to package directions. Next, cut out a fabric strip and starch it.

Set the serger for a chain stitch. Insert the binding fabric into the binder accessory; the wrong side of the fabric should face the left. Feed the fabric under the presser foot as you begin stitching.

The fabric that is to be bound is then inserted in the double fold bias binder. As you stitch, the fabric will be encased with the binding.

The Double Fold Bias Binder

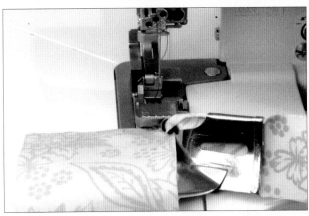

The Binder in Action
The binder fabric is fed through the double fold bias binder before it's stitched into place.

Finished Binding
Compare the looper (or bottom) side of the binding (top piece) with the needle (or right) side of the binding (bottom piece).

What's Your Width?

The double fold bias binder accessory comes in different widths. Check your manual to determine the width of fabric strips to use with your binder.

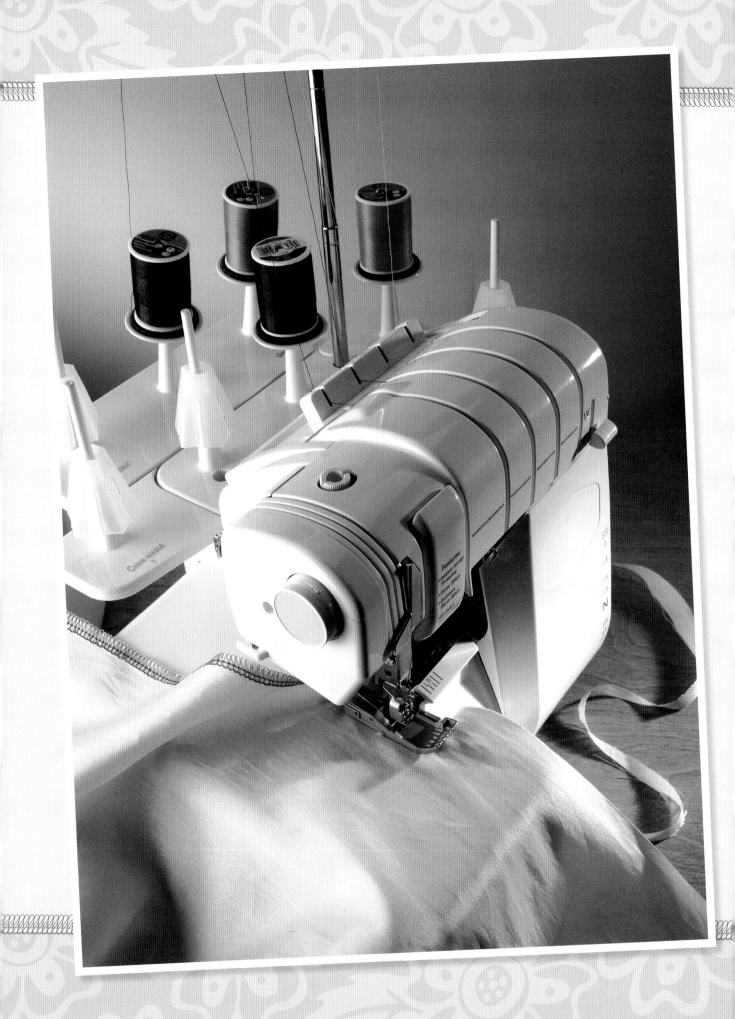

2

Stitching With Your Serger

Now that you've conquered your serger fears, it's time to get acquainted with that wonderful little machine and learn what it is capable of. You will also become familiar with all those extras that will enhance your serging experiences.

Get out your fabric scraps and start serging, as we explore the stitch variations available on many sergers and how those stitches may be adjusted. In no time at all you will be as familiar with your serger and the serging tools as you are with your sewing machine and your favorite sewing notions.

Notions and Tools

As with every job or hobby, there are tools of the trade that make the job easier or help enhance your project. Serging is no different. Here are a few notions and tools I find essential.

Thread

Thread manufactured specifically for the serger is lighter weight than all-purpose sewing thread. Because you will be using multiple spools of thread when you serge, purchase three or four spools of the basic colors that you will be using most often.

When the fabric for your serger project is a nontraditional color, use a basic thread color that comes as close as possible to matching the fabric for the loopers and the right needle. For the left needle, use a matching serger thread or even a matching all-purpose thread. Remember, the needle threads are the only ones that penetrate the fabric. The left needle creates the seam line, so that thread is the only one that shows in the seam line.

From the Handy to the Essential
There are many notions and tools that will make your serging experience easier and more enjoyable.

Decorative threads are like icing on the cake. The way the wonderful textures combine with the decorative colors allows you to enhance your projects in beautiful ways. The stepped-up versions of the projects in this book provide a wonderful opportunity for you to test out some of the decorative serger threads that are available.

Threads, Threads and More Threads
From basic serger threads (above left) to decorative threads (above right), a wide range of colors and textures is available.

Painter's Tape

Painter's tape is similar to masking tape but does not leave a sticky residue. I often use it in serging projects where I need to attach elements together but I don't want to use pins. You can purchase painter's tape wherever you purchase painting supplies.

Thread Nets

Thread nets are essential when working with decorative threads, which are so slick they just slide off the spool and puddle around the thread pin. Consequently, the threads get tangled up and break. The thread net eliminates this since the threads will puddle in the net. See the sidebar at right for instructions.

Tweezers

Sergers generally come with a pair of tweezers. On many models, the tweezers are needed to thread the serger. Tweezers are also handy for moving threads or thread tails behind the needles.

Looper/Needle Threader

Many sergers require a looper threader to thread the lower looper. A looper threader may be similar to a needle threader, or it may have a hook on the end. With a little practice, it's easy to use.

Some sergers come with built-in needle threaders. With these, the needles must be in the correct position for the threader to work. Usually there are placement marks on the hand wheel to indicate the correct position.

If your serger has a needle threader you will want to check your manual for needle threader instructions.

As my eyes get older, I find needle threaders more and more beneficial.

Using a Thread Net

A thread net is easy to use. Simply insert one end of the thread net into the hole in the bottom of the spool (photo *A*). Fold the other end of the net up and around the bottom of the spool (photo *B*).

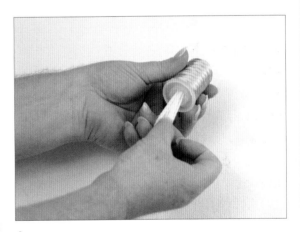

A

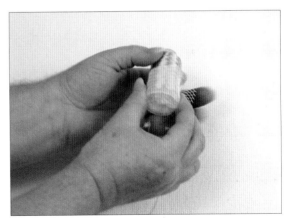

B

Hiding Thread Tails
Use the double-eyed needle to tuck unsightly thread tails into stitches where they won't be seen.

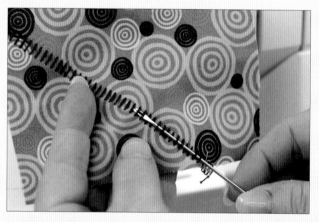

Inserting Ribbon
The double-eyed needle serves as a bodkin for threading ribbon through decorative stitches.

A Lint Brush and Canned Air

With each stitch you make, you're cutting off small amounts of fabrics or threads that often find their way down into the workings of your serger. Keeping the inside of your serger clean is essential, so purchase a small thread or lint brush and use it often.

Also, you will find that you can't do without canned air to keep the inside of your machine free of lint and threads. The canned air comes with a straw that directs the spray into small areas that your lint brush can't reach.

Seam Sealant

Seam sealant is a clear liquid that prevents threads or fabric from raveling. Usually the sealant dries clear, but I recommend doing a test on a sample piece of fabric if the sealant will be used in a conspicuous spot. Seam sealant can be stiff when it dries, so be careful not use too much in the area of a project that will be next to the skin.

Double-Eyed Needle

At first glance, the double-eyed needle appears to have a manufacturer's defect. Both ends of the needle have an eye, with no sharp point to penetrate the fabric.

The double-eyed needle is used to tuck thread tails under a serged seam. (See page 30 for more on thread tails.) You can also use it to thread narrow ribbon under decorative stitches.

Some Serger Stitching Basics

Stitch Length and Width

Many sergers allow you to make adjustments to the stitches. One of these is adjusting the stitch length.

The stitch length is the distance from one needle penetration to the next. As a general rule, I set a stitch length of 2.5–3.0mm (about ⅛") for most of my serging projects. But as in sewing, you will want to adjust the length of stitches from time to time. I find that most of my stitch length variations come in decorative elements or special techniques.

When using decorative threads, the size of the thread can require adjusting the stitch length. If you are using a very fine thread, you may need a shorter stitch length to achieve the desired effects. However, if the thread is heavy or bulky, you would need to increase the stitch

length or your seam would not lie flat—it would have too much bulk.

Another adjustment is to the stitch width, which is the distance from the cut edge of the fabric to the needle (or to the left needle if you are using two needles). Typically I set a stitch width of 6.0mm (about ¼"), which is a perfect seam allowance for garments or quilt piecing. If I am creating a project with a heavy fabric (e.g., wool or denim) I will generally increase the width of my stitches to the maximum that my serger will stitch. At the same time, if I am using a very lightweight fabric I will decrease the stitch width.

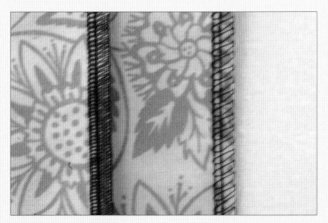

The Effects of Stitch Length
Shortening the stitch length (left) allows for more thread coverage, while lengthening the stitch length (right) lessens the bulk of the seam.

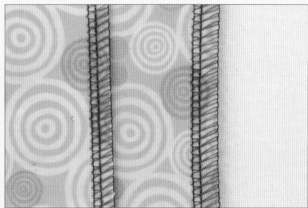

The Effects of Stitch Width
A narrow seam width (left) is perfect for small projects such as doll clothes or baby garments, but you will find that a wider seam (right) gives the best results for most projects.

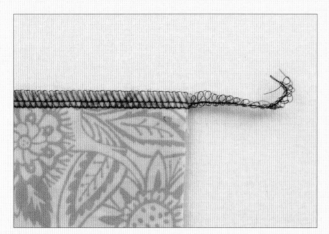

Thread Tail

Tucking Thread Tail Back Into Seam

Thread Tails

When you finish a seam on your sewing machine, you stop at the edge of the fabric. Not so with a serger. The preferred action is to *stitch off*, which means that you continue to serge beyond the fabric's edge until you have a *thread tail* that is long enough for you to cut.

If you are going to serge over this seam with another seam, don't worry about finishing off the tail. However, if the thread tail is not going to be stitched over, you should *finish* this seam.

One way is to tuck the tail back into the serged seam. Thread the tail through one of the eyes of a double-eyed needle and run the needle under the loops of the serged seam.

Another option is to clip the threads and apply seam sealant. This finish is perfectly fine on an area that will not have a lot of wear and tear. Keep in mind that some of the seam sealants harden when they dry.

Wrapping Corners

Serger seams tend to be bulkier than those created on a sewing machine. When your sewing projects have corners, usually you can clip the corners to reduce bulk. However, if you clip serged corners, your stitches will fall out, leaving a hole in your project.

Wrapping the corners is a technique that reduces the bulk (and works with both the serger and the sewing machine):

1. Serge one of the seams that will be meeting at the corner.
2. Fold or press the serged seam allowance to one side, along the needle line.
3. With the previous seam allowance folded under, serge the perpendicular edge, enclosing the first seam allowance in the second seam.

Wrapped Corner

SERGER HOW-TO: Removing Stitches

It can be a bit intimidating when you look at a serged seam that needs to be removed. Put your fears aside. You have only to remove the needle thread; the looper threads then will fall away. Here is the easiest way to accomplish the task.

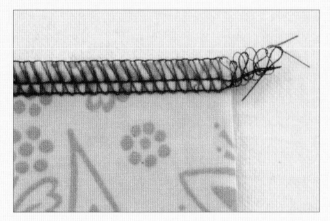

1 Cut the serger tail off at about ½" (1cm) from the edge of the fabric.

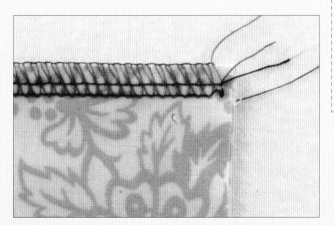

2 Straighten out the threads in the serger tail. You will have 2 long threads and a short thread for each needle used in the stitch.

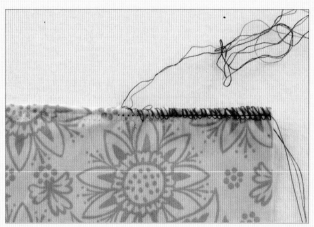

3 Pull the needle threads (the short threads) as if you were creating gathers in the fabric. As you pull out the needle threads, the looper threads will fall away.

A Ripping Good Alternative

If your stitch length is very short, or if your fabric is stiff or bulky, the needle threads can be difficult to pull out. When that happens, use your seam ripper. Remember, rip only the needle threads; the loopers will fall away when the needle threads are no longer holding them in place.

Pressing Serged Seams

Pressing is the key to beautiful project construction. Whether you are sewing or serging, you can never press too much.

Here are a few tips:

* When you have completed a seam, press the seam flat, then press it to one side.
* For a craft project, press the seams in the direction that will create the least amount of bulk.
* If you're making a garment, press the seams toward the back of the garment.
* A serged seam tends to fold naturally to the lower looper side. Knowing this will allow you to plan ahead as you serge. The fabric that is on the bottom or next to the throat plate is the fabric that will be on the lower looper side. Since the seam tends to fold in this direction, your seams will press easier to the fabric next to the throat plate.

Offset Seams

Another way to reduce bulk in your projects is to offset the seam allowance, i.e., press seam allowances in opposite directions. If you have ever quilted, this will make perfect sense, as quilters generally prefer their seam allowances to go in opposite directions.

For those of you who are not quilters and are more familiar with sewing techniques, offsetting the seams is the serger equivalent to pressing your seams open. When you press your seams open, half the bulk of the seam allowance goes to each side of the seam.

With serging, you can't press the seams open. You will press one serged seam allowance to the left and the other to the right, offsetting the seam allowances. When you do this in an area where you have joined seams, your results will be similar to pressing the seams open in sewing.

Lining Up Seams
In addition to reducing bulk, offsetting the seams also makes it much easier to line up the seams.

A Guide To Favorite Stitches

The 3-Thread Overlock Stitch

This stitch is created with one needle thread and an upper and lower looper thread. It's used to finish a seam that won't require a lot of wear and tear; it's also used when more stretch is desired.

In a perfectly balanced 3-thread overlock stitch, the upper and lower looper threads meet at the edge of the fabric, lying flat and looping around the needle thread. The needle thread lays a straight line of stitching on the top of the fabric, with little-to-no needle thread showing on the back.

The 4-Thread Overlock Stitch

This is the stitch I use most often. It's created with two needle threads and an upper and lower looper thread. Use this stitch when you want a durable finished seam.

In a perfectly balanced 4-thread overlock stitch, the upper and lower looper threads meet at the edge of the fabric, lying flat and looping around the left needle thread. The needle threads lie in straight lines of stitching on the top of the fabric, with little-to-no needle threads showing on the back.

Seam Using the 3-Thread Overlock Stitch

Seam Using the 4-Thread Overlock Stitch

The Rolled Edge Stitch

This is a wonderful stitch to use as a decorative hem or to finish seams on sheer or lightweight fabric. The rolled edge stitch can be created with two threads (one needle and one looper) or three threads (one needle and two loopers). Refer to your manual to determine if your serger makes a 2- or 3-thread rolled edge or if your serger can make both stitches. I personally like the 3-thread rolled edge for most applications.

If you're using the rolled edge stitch for seams, generally you will use standard serger thread in the loopers and needle. If you're using the rolled edge stitch for decorative hems, use standard thread in the needle and in the lower looper. Since the upper looper is the thread that wraps around the edge, this thread should be decorative.

Decorative Hem Using the Rolled Edge Stitch

The Flatlock Stitch

This is another great stitch that can be used for seaming fabrics together or for decorative purposes. The flatlock stitch can be created with two, three or four threads. Refer to your manual for threading instructions specific to your serger.

When joining bulky fabrics that don't ravel, the flatlock stitch is a great choice because it allows the seams to lie flat, with the seam allowance encased inside the stitches.

If you want the bars to show on the right side of the fabric, serge with the right sides of the fabric together. If you want the loops to show on the right side of the fabric, serge with the wrong sides of the fabric together.

This stitch is not recommended for high-stress seams.

Bars and Loops

If you open one side of the flatlock stitch, you'll see bars that resemble the rungs of a ladder. The opposite side of the stitch shows the loops.

To show the **bars** on the right side of the fabric, serge with the right sides of the fabric pieces together. To show the **loops** on the right side of the fabric, serge with the wrong sides of the fabric pieces together.

Creating a Flatlock Seam

1. Trim away all but about ³⁄₁₆" (5mm) of the seam allowance.

2. Stitch the fabric pieces together, guiding the edge of the fabric between the needle and the cutting blade. You want the stitches to hang off the edge of the fabric.

3. Open the fabrics and manipulate them until the encased seam allowances lie flat.

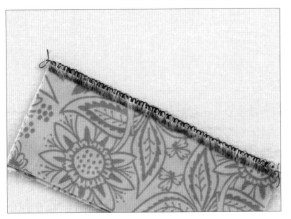

Flatlock Seam
The loops hanging off the edge of the seam allow the seam to lie flat when the fabric pieces are opened.

Using the Flatlock Stitch as a Decorative Element

If you want to create a decorative element with the 2-thread flatlock stitch, you can use a standard thread and one decorative thread. The placement of the threads will depend on the look you want to achieve.

For decorative bars, thread the needle with decorative thread and serge with the right sides of the fabric together. For decorative loops, thread the looper with decorative thread and serge with the wrong sides of the fabric together.

How to do it:

1. Fold the fabric along the line where you want to add the decorative element. Make sure you know whether to fold the fabric with right sides together or wrong sides together, depending on the look you want to achieve.

2. Stitch along the fold line, remembering to let the stitches hang off the edge.

3. Open the fabric and press flat.

The Look You Want
Create decorative bars (example on left) or decorative loops (example on right).

The Chain Stitch

Many sergers are capable of making a chain stitch. The chain stitch is created with one needle and one looper thread. The needle side of the stitch looks like a straight line of stitching created on a sewing machine. The looper side of the chain stitch is a row of loops.

This stitch can be used for seams and for creating decorative elements on your fabric. (For decorative elements, you will have to lower or turn off the upper looper. Check your manual to see if your serger has this capability.)

When used as a seam, the serged chain stitch has more stretch than a seam created on a sewing machine, but it is not as stable. The chain stitch can unravel easily simply by pulling the right thread (see sidebar).

When using the chain stitch to create a decorative element, use standard serger thread in the needle and a decorative thread in the looper. Stitch from the wrong side of the fabric. When you have completed the row of stitching, turn your fabric over to see the decorative loops.

The Chain Stitch
The example on the right shows the straight line appearance of the chain stitch. The example on the left shows the underside of the stitch, which is a row of loops.

Unraveling the Chain Stitch

When you want to unravel the chain stitch, the *right* thread to pull is the looper thread at the end of the seam (not at the beginning).

You will also need to unloop the looper thread from the needle thread. To do this, turn the fabric over to the needle side and pull the needle thread out of a couple of stitches. Turn the fabric back to the looper side and give that thread a pull.

The Cover Stitch

The cover stitch is available on some models of sergers and on cover stitch-only machines. Check your manual—and consider yourself lucky if you have a serger that includes this stitch.

It's similar to the chain stitch, with one looper thread. However, the cover stitch uses two or three needles instead of the one needle used in the chain stitch.

The Cover Stitch
Serging on the right side of the fabric results in parallel rows of stitches (example on left). To create decorative looper stitches (example on right), serge on the wrong side of the fabric.

The cover stitch has two or three parallel lines of stitching on the needle side of the fabric. The underside of the fabric shows loops between the rows of stitching. The cover stitch can be used for seams, decorative elements and hemming.

Using the cover stitch for seams has the same pros and cons as using the chain stitch. You'll wind up with a stretch seam that can easily unravel if the right thread is pulled.

As with the chain stitch, the *right* thread to pull in the cover stitch is the final end of the looper thread. Remove

Hemming with the Cover Stitch

My favorite use for the cover stitch is hemming. The cover stitch results in a stretch hem that's perfect for knits. If you have a knit garment, likely it was hemmed with a cover stitch.

How to do it:

1. Turn the hem under and press (no need to finish the edge).

2. Thread the looper and the needles with standard serger thread.

3. Stitch with the garment right side up and the needles on either side of the turned-under fabric edge. The raw edge will be encased in the loops (see the left example in the photo).

the needle threads from a couple of stitches, then pull the looper thread.

With so many beautiful threads that can be used for decorative stitching, you will love incorporating these into the cover stitch. Thread the needles with standard serger thread and the looper with a decorative thread. Sew from the wrong side of the fabric so that the decorative thread loops appear on the right side of the fabric.

Stitching Straight Lines

Way back when I was in school, I learned that a straight line is the shortest distance between two points. Think of your desire to serge as *Point A* and a finished project as *Point B*. Now, let's move straight ahead and reach *Point B* in the shortest amount of time possible.

How do we do that? With a straight line, of course. In this chapter you will find projects that use only a straight stitch—no curves, no turns, just a straight line. In a matter of minutes, you will have completed your first project.

Relax! Serger success is *straight* ahead.

Fabric for this project provided by P&B Textiles from their Linden collection.

MATERIALS LIST

* ½ yard (46cm) fabric
* Coordinating serger thread

SERGER SETTINGS

4-Thread Overlock
Stitch Length: 3mm (⅛")
Stitch Width: M or ¼" (6mm)
Cutting Blade: ON
Serger Thread: Standard
Foot: Standard

SEAM ALLOWANCE

¼" (6mm)

cord cover

Quick and easy describes the cord cover. Within minutes you will have completed your first serger project *and* you will have enjoyed it. In fact, you may find yourself making covers for all the electrical cords in your home—then for seasons and holidays, friends and family…the list goes on and on.

Your serger will get a workout making these cord covers—and your serger confidence will get a power surge!

Basic Project Instructions

1 Cut 3 strips of fabric each measuring 5" × 36" (13cm × 91cm). (This size will work for a cord that is about 6 feet [1.8m] in length.)

2 Place the right sides of the 3 fabric strips together. Then, using a ¼" (6mm) seam, serge the strips together along the 5" (13cm) edges, creating a single strip of fabric that measures 5" × 107" (13cm × 2.7m).

3 Serge along the raw edges of both of the 5" (13cm) ends.

4 Fold the strip of fabric in half lengthwise, with the right sides of the fabric together, and serge the 107" (2.7m) edges together using a ¼" (6mm) seam.

5 Turn the tube of fabric right side out and press along the seam line. Thread the cord into the cord cover. Tuck the serged edges into the cord cover and evenly space the gathers.

It's All About the Length

For different lengths of cords, multiply the measurement of the cord by 2 to get the finished length. The width of your fabric will be determined by how many 5" (13cm) strips you'll need for a cord of the desired length.

Fabric for this project provided by P&B Textiles from their Linden collection.

MATERIALS LIST

* ½ yard (46cm) fabric
* Coordinating serger thread
* Decorative thread

SERGER SETTINGS

Settings vary in Steps 2 and 3.

4-Thread Overlock
Stitch Length: 3mm (⅛")
Stitch Width: M or ¼" (6mm)
Cutting Blade: ON
Serger Thread: Standard
Foot: Standard

SEAM ALLOWANCE

¼" (6mm)

stepped-up
cord cover

Now that you've mastered the cord cover, you can *step it up* a bit by adding a rolled edge to the ends. This gives a nice finished hem and allows you to experiment with some of the wonderful decorative threads that are available.

This stitch combined with fabulous thread makes a wonderful hem; that's why I've included it in many of the *stepped up* projects in this book. I'm sure you'll love this stitch as much as I do.

Stepped-Up Project Instructions

1 Cut 3 strips of fabric each measuring 5" × 36" (13cm × 91cm). With the right sides of 2 strips facing, serge the strips together along the 5" (13cm) edges using a ¼" seam. Repeat, serging the third strip to the first 2, creating a single strip of fabric that measures 5" × 107" (13cm × 2.7m).

SERGER SETTINGS
(STEP 2)

3-Thread Rolled Edge

Stitch Length: 1.5mm (¹⁄₁₆")

Stitch Width: ⅛" (3.5mm)

Cutting Blade: ON

Serger Thread: Standard, in needle and lower looper

Decorative Thread: In upper looper

Foot: Standard

SERGER SETTINGS
(STEP 3)

4-Thread Overlock

Stitch Length: 3mm (⅛")

Stitch Width: M or ¼" (6mm)

Cutting Blade: ON

Serger Thread: Standard

Foot: Standard

3 Fold the strip of fabric in half lengthwise, right sides facing, and serge the 107" (2.7m) edges together using a ¼" (6mm) seam.

4 Turn the tube of fabric right side out and press along the seam line. Thread the cord into the cord cover and evenly space the gathers along the cord.

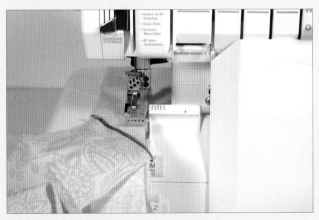

2 Using the rolled edge stitch, hem the raw edges of both of the 5" (13cm) ends.

Fabric for this project provided by P&B Textiles from their Linden collection.

MATERIALS LIST

* ⅙ yard (15cm) Fabric *A* (rice bag)
* ⅙ yard (15cm) Fabric *B* (bag cover)
* 2–3 cups (.5–.7L) rice
* Coordinating serger thread

SERGER SETTINGS

4-Thread Overlock
Stitch Length: 3mm (⅛")
Stitch Width: M or ¼" (6mm)
Cutting Blade: ON
Serger Thread: Standard
Foot: Standard

SEAM ALLOWANCE

¼" (6mm)

rice bag

My oldest son has been playing rugby since he became an adult and didn't need Mom's permission to be on the team. Needless to say, he comes home with aches and pains on a regular basis. I often find him, with a new black eye, digging around my sewing room for a rice bag. Heating the bag 1½ to 2 minutes in the microwave is perfect for his rugby aches and pains, and it should be just right for your aches and pains as well.

Basic Project Instructions

1 Cut two 5" × 42" (13cm × 107cm) rectangles, 1 from Fabric *A* and 1 from Fabric *B*.

2 Fold Fabric *A* in half lengthwise, right sides together, and stitch along both side seams, leaving the 5" (13cm) end open. Turn right side out and press flat.

3 Mark fold/seam lines every 5" (13cm) on the right side of Fabric *A*.

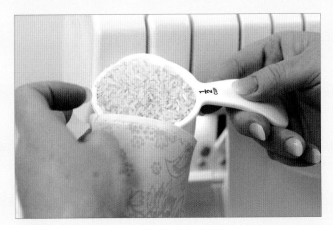

4 Pour ½–⅔ cup (118–156ml) of rice into the rice bag.

5 Turn off or disengage the serger's cutting blade. Fold the bag along the fold/seam line closest to the rice and serge along the fold.

6 Repeat the process of adding ½–⅔ cup (118–156 ml) of rice and stitching along the fold line 2 more times.

7 Add the final ½–⅔ cup (118–156ml) of rice and fold ⅓" (8mm) of the cut edge to one side. Serge the bottom of the bag closed along this fold line.

Sewing the Rice Bag Cover

The rice bag will be used often; it will need to be cleaned often, too. Since rice does not launder well, a removable cover is a necessity. With all the wonderful fabrics available, you can make the removable cover to match the personality of the person who will be using the bag.

1 Turn the cutting blade on.

2 Serge to finish each 5" (13cm) end of the cover. With wrong sides facing, press 2" (5cm) of one end under.

4 Serge the side seams.

3 With wrong sides facing, fold the bag cover, overlapping the pressed-under edge and the opposite end approximately 2" (5cm).

5 Turn the cover right side out through the overlapped opening and press. Insert the rice bag into the cover.

Evenly Distributing the Rice

You can easily distribute the rice within the cover by stuffing the bag into one end, then hold the bag and cover up together and shake. This will allow the rice bag to shift to the bottom of the cover.

MATERIALS LIST

* ⅙ yard (15cm) Fabric *A* (rice bag)
* ⅙ yard (15cm) Fabric *B*
  (bag cover back)
* ¼ yard (23cm) Fabric *C*
  (bag cover front)
* ¼ yard (23cm) Fabric *D*
  (bag cover front)
* 2–3 cups (.5–.7L) rice
* Coordinating serger thread

SERGER SETTINGS

4-Thread Overlock
Stitch Length: 3mm (⅛")
Stitch Width: M or ¼" (6mm)
Cutting Blade: ON
Serger Thread: Standard
Foot: Standard

SEAM ALLOWANCE

¼" (6mm)

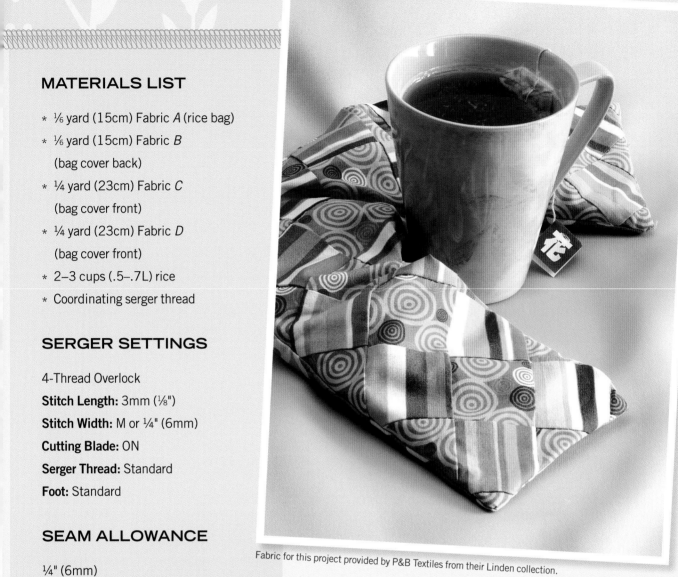

Fabric for this project provided by P&B Textiles from their Linden collection.

stepped-up
rice bag

I love to learn new quilting techniques, but I find that I don't always have time to complete a quilt. This stepped-up removable cover for the rice bag is a wonderful opportunity to practice piecing with your serger.

You may enjoy this so much that your next quilt (or first quilt) just might be a serger project.

Stepped-Up Project Instructions

1 Cut the fabric as follows:
  * Cut a 5" × 42" (13cm × 107cm) rectangle from Fabric *A* for the rice bag.
  * Cut two 5" × 12" (13cm × 30cm) rectangles from Fabric *B* for the back of the cover.
  * Cut 3 strips 2¼" × 42" (6cm × 107cm) from Fabric *C* for the pieced front.
  * Cut 2 strips 2¼" × 42" (6cm × 107cm) from Fabric *D* for the pieced front.

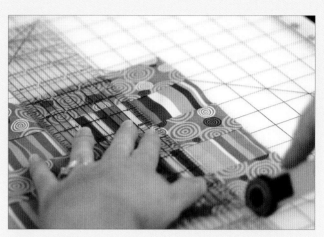

2 Sew the rice bag from the Fabric *A* rectangle following steps 1–7 on page 45.

4 Cut eleven 2¼" (6cm) strips from the pieced panel.

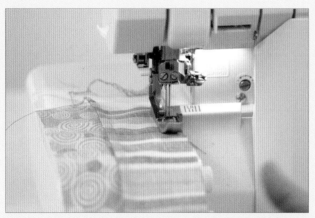

3 Serge one Fabric *C* strip to one Fabric *D* strip along the 42" (107cm) sides. Press the seams toward the Fabric *C* strip. Serging will be easier if you press the seam toward the fabric that's on the bottom, next to the throat plate.

  Continue to serge the strips together until all 5 strips are connected, creating a panel.

5 With right sides facing, serge 2 of the pieced strips, offsetting the ends/seams so that Fabric *C* blocks are sewn to Fabric *D* blocks .

8 With right sides facing, serge the back pieces to the front panel at each 5" (13cm) end. Finish the ends of the back pieces by serging each end separately.

6 Continue to add the pieced strips until all 11 strips have been sewn together to create a panel.

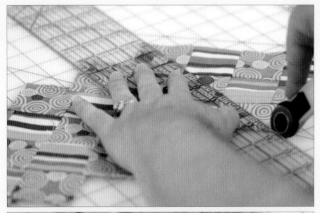

9 With wrong sides together, press 2" (5cm) of 1 back end piece under. Fold the back pieces over the front, overlapping the folded edge closest to the front.

10 Serge the front to the back along both side seams. Turn right side out through the over-lapped opening in the cover and press. Insert the rice bag into the cover.

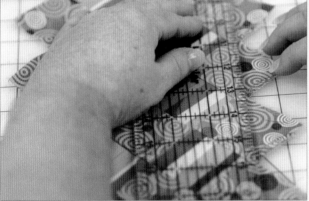

7 Cut the 5" × 20" (13cm × 51cm) front of the bag cover out of the pieced panel.

Fabric for this project provided by P&B Textiles from their Linden collection.

MATERIALS LIST

* 8½" × 13" (22cm × 33cm) quilted fabric
* 12" (30cm) zipper (no metal teeth)
* Coordinating serger thread

SERGER SETTINGS

4-Thread Overlock
Stitch Length: 3mm (⅛")
Stitch Width: M or ¼" (6mm)
Cutting Blade: ON
Serger Thread: Standard
Foot: Cording

SEAM ALLOWANCE

¼" (6mm)

cosmetic bag

This project has been a favorite in my serging classes for as long as I have taught. Class participants are always amazed at how quick and easy it is to make this useful little bag. By using a cording foot and your 4-thread overlock stitch, you will complete this project with four little seams.

Warning: This project is so fast and fun, you may not want to stop with just one. Start gathering zippers!

Basic Project Instructions

1 Cut one 8½" × 13" (22cm × 33cm) rectangle from the quilted fabric.

2 Open the zipper and center it, right sides together, along one 8½" (22cm) end of the quilted fabric. (The zipper will be about 1" [3cm] longer than the fabric on each end.)

3 Serge the edge of the zipper to the end of the bag, lining up the teeth of the zipper in the groove of the cording foot.

4 Close the zipper and make fabric placement marks to indicate where the zipper lines up with the edge of the fabric.

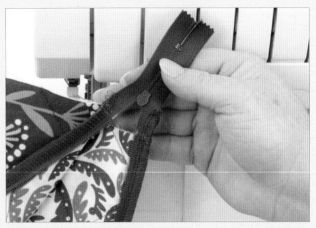

5 Open the zipper. On the opposite end of the bag, with the right sides of the zipper together, align with the fabric placement marks and serge the zipper to the fabric. Close the zipper and press flat.

6 Fold the bag with the zipper 1" (3cm) below the top fold of the bag.

7 Serge along the edge of the bag, right sides together, where the bottom of the zipper is located, cutting off the excess zipper.

8 Open the zipper about 2" (5cm). Serge along the side of the bag where the top of the zipper is positioned, cutting off the excess zipper.

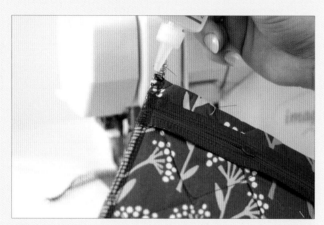

9 Secure all 4 corners of the bag with a seam sealant.

10 Turn the bag right side out through the open zipper. Press the bag and enjoy!

MATERIALS LIST

* 8½" × 13" (22cm × 33cm) quilted fabric
* 12" (30cm) zipper (no metal teeth)
* Coordinating serger thread
* Decorative thread

SERGER SETTINGS

Settings vary in Step 2.

4-Thread Overlock
Stitch Length: 3mm (⅛")
Stitch Width: M or ¼" (6mm)
Cutting Blade: ON
Serger Thread: Standard
Foot: Cording

SEAM ALLOWANCE

¼" (6mm)

Fabric for this project provided by P&B Textiles from their Linden collection.

stepped-up
cosmetic bag

Get out your decorative threads, because we are going to step up the zipper on this project. By adding a tassel to the zipper on this little bag, we will not only make it easier to open, but we will also add a little personality to an already great project.

1 Create the cosmetic bag by following the directions on pages 50–52.

SERGER SETTINGS
(STEP 2)

Chain Stitch

Stitch Length: 3mm (⅛")

Stitch Width: M or ¼" (6mm)

Cutting Blade: OFF

Decorative Thread: In needle and chain looper

Foot: Standard

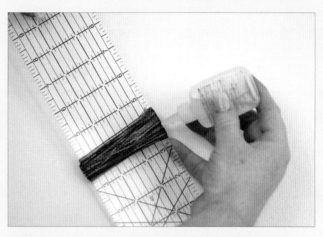

3 Wrap 8 yards (7.3m) of the chain around a 3" (8cm) ruler or piece of cardboard. Apply a seam sealant to one edge of the wrapped chain. (This edge will be cut after the seam sealant dries.)

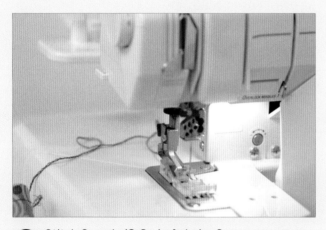

2 Stitch 9 yards (8.2m) of chain. On many sergers you will have to start the chain while stitching on a small piece of fabric, but once the stitch has begun, you will be able to stitch without fabric.

A Nice Substitute

If you don't have a chain stitch on your serger, you will get similar results by setting your serger to a rolled hem.

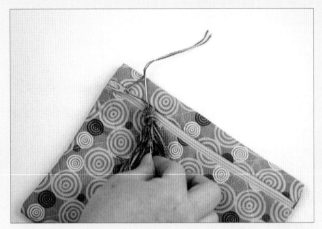

4 Tie the wrapped loops that do not have seam sealant on them together with about 10" (25cm) of the remaining yard of chain. Be sure not to cut the ends of the knot off, as they will be used to tie the tassel to the zipper in a later step.

7 Tie the tassel to the pull of the zipper by slipping 1 end of the tassel knot through the opening in the zipper pull. Use the double-eyed needle to thread the end of the tie through the tassel, then tie the ends where they can be hidden within the tassel.

5 Slide the chain off of the ruler or cardboard and cut the loops where the seam sealant has dried.

8 If the tied ends are longer than the tassel, trim them to the tassel length and add a small amount of seam sealant to the cut threads.

6 Wrap the tied ends of the tassel with the remaining piece of chain. Tie it off and hide the knot in the tassel.

Fabric for this project provided by P&B Textiles from their Linden collection.

MATERIALS LIST

* 26" × 40" (66cm × 102cm)
  Fabric *A* (pillowcase)
* 10" × 40" (25cm × 102cm)
  Fabric *B* (band)
* Coordinating serger thread

SERGER SETTINGS

4-Thread Overlock
Stitch Length: 3mm (⅛")
Stitch Width: M or ¼" (6mm)
Cutting Blade: ON
Serger Thread: Standard
Foot: Standard

SEAM ALLOWANCE

¼" (6mm)

pillowcase

One of the joys of sewing for your children is seeing the pleasure and appreciation in their eyes. My boys, now past their teens, still love to have pillowcases made by Mom. It brings me joy to see those big ole boys running through the fabric store searching for just the right fabric. Let the teenagers in your life pick out fabric for their own pillowcases. You, too, will see that pleasure and appreciation that warms a mother's heart.

Basic Project Instructions

1 Create the body of the pillowcase by folding Fabric *A*, right sides together, and serging the 26" (66cm) side seam.

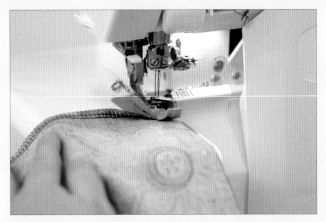

2 Serge the bottom of the pillowcase, right sides together, "wrapping" the side seam as you serge over it (see "Wrapping Corners" on page 30).

3 Create the band for the pillowcase by folding Fabric *B*, right sides together, and serging the 10" (25cm) side seam.

4 Fold the band in half lengthwise, wrong sides together, and press.

5 Line up all side seams and the raw edges of the pillowcase and the band. Serge through all layers.

6 Fold band out and press.

Fabric for this project provided by P&B Textiles from their Linden collection.

MATERIALS LIST

* 26" × 40" (66cm × 102cm) Fabric *A* (pillowcase)
* Two 10" × 42" (25cm × 107cm) Fabric *B* (ruffle)
* Coordinating serger thread
* Decorative thread

SERGER SETTINGS

Settings vary in Step 7.

4-Thread Overlock
Stitch Length: 3mm (⅛")
Stitch Width: M or ¼" (6mm)
Cutting Blade: ON
Serger Thread: Standard
Foot: Standard

SEAM ALLOWANCE

¼" (6mm)

stepped-up
pillowcase

I have lovingly crafted superhero, cartoon character and sports team pillowcases for the boys in my life. But I have to confess: My favorite pillowcases are ruffled. For me, choosing a beautiful fabric and adding a flowing ruffle is what pillowcases are all about. I guess the femininity of the ruffle helps balance the masculinity of having a house full of males. So get out your ruffler foot and add a little femininity to your pillowcases.

Stepped-Up Project Instructions

1 Serge the 2 Fabric *B* pieces, right sides together, creating a 10" × 80" (25cm × 203cm) length of fabric for a ruffle.

2 Attach the ruffler foot to the serger.

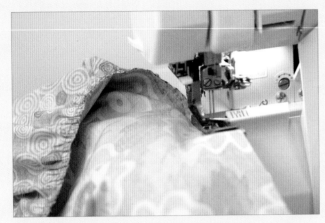

3 With right sides together, serge the ruffle fabric and the pillowcase fabric, gathering the ruffle as it is attached to the pillow case.

4 Trim the side seams of the pillowcase and the ruffle, creating a straight edge.

5 With right sides together, match the seam between the ruffle and the pillowcase and serge the side seam. With the right sides together, serge the bottom of the pillowcase.

6 Turn the pillowcase right side out and press the side and bottom seams.

SERGER SETTINGS
(STEP 7)

3-Thread Rolled Edge

Stitch Length: 1.5mm (¹⁄₁₆")
Stitch Width: ⅛" (3.5mm)
Cutting Blade: ON
Serger Thread: Standard, in needle and lower looper
Decorative Thread: In upper looper
Foot: Standard

7 With the rolled edge stitch, hem the edge of the pillowcase ruffle. Tuck the serger tail under the rolled edge with a double-eyed needle.

When Your Fabrics Are Uneven

Your fabrics probably will not end up exactly even. If the ruffle is longer than the pillowcase, simply trim off the excess in step 4. Likewise, if the pillowcase is no more than 2" (5cm) longer than the ruffle, you can trim off the excess. Be careful, though, as trimming more than 2" (5cm) off of the pillowcase may make it too snug for your pillow.

Layering Fabric

By now you are a master of straight-line serging, and you have created some great projects using your newfound skills. In fact, I bet you could serge a straight line with your eyes closed.

But don't close your eyes just yet; you'll want to keep them wide open for all of the exciting new techniques you'll encounter in this chapter. In addition to new techniques, you will be creating these great projects with little to no pinning. I know that when you learned to sew, pinning fabric was a very important step. However, pins and the cutting blade on your serger do not work well together. Learning to control multiple layers of fabric without pins as you serge is key to serger success.

Before you know it you'll be able to layer fabric, serging straight seams and turning the fabric this way and that to create a variety of projects in just a matter of minutes!

Fabric for this project provided by P&B Textiles from their Linden collection.

MATERIALS LIST

* 5" × 6" (13cm × 15cm)
  Fabric *A* (card holder)
* Two 5" × 5" (13cm × 13cm)
  Fabric *B* (card holder pockets)
* 5" × 5" (13cm × 13cm)
  Fabric *C* (card holder lining)
* 5" (13cm) length of stretch
  grosgrain ribbon
* Coordinating serger thread
* Painter's tape

SERGER SETTINGS

4-Thread Overlock
Stitch Length: 3.5mm (⅛")
Stitch Width: M or ¼" (6mm)
Cutting Blade: ON
Serger Thread: Standard
Foot: Standard

SEAM ALLOWANCE

¼" (6mm)

business card holder

When I travel, I meet wonderful people with whom I want to keep in contact. I carry business cards, but I could never locate them as I dug around my bag. Finally I'd write my information on any scrap of paper I could find.

Then a dear friend gave me my own business card holder. You wouldn't believe how helpful it is! If you're like me and need a little extra help organizing your business cards, this project is a life saver.

Basic Project Instructions

1 Cut out all fabric pieces as indicated in the Materials List on page 62.

2 Fold the Fabric *B* pieces in half, wrong sides together, and press.

3 Align one pocket piece to one end of Fabric *A*, right sides together, and serge the pocket to the card holder. Repeat for the other pocket piece, serging to the opposite end of Fabric *A* with right sides together.

4 Fold the pocket pieces away from the center piece. Using painter's tape, affix the stretch ribbon in position as shown in the photo. After you have taped the ribbon in place, fold the pocket pieces over the center piece.

Sharpen Your Corners

Wrapping the corners will make them sharper when the card case is turned right side out. See page 30 for directions for this technique.

5 Place Fabric *C* on top of the pocket and outside pieces, right sides together, and serge along the side seams, wrapping the pocket seams as you serge over them. (The lining will not extend all the way to the top and bottom of the outside piece.)

6 Turn the lining right side out. Fold both pockets to the lining side of the card case. Remove the painter's tape.

7 Press all the edges flat. Put your business cards into the pockets. To close the card case, fold it and wrap the stretch ribbon around the outside.

Fabric for this project provided by P&B Textiles from their Linden collection.

MATERIALS LIST

* 7" × 8" (18cm × 20cm)
  Fabric *A* (card holder)
* Two 5" × 5" (13cm × 13cm)
  Fabric *B* (card holder pockets)
* 5" × 5" (13cm × 13cm)
  Fabric *C* (card holder lining)
* ½ yard (46cm) length of
  ⅛" (3mm) ribbon
* 5" (13cm) length of stretch
  grosgrain ribbon
* Coordinating serger thread
* Decorative thread

SERGER SETTINGS

2-Thread Flatlock
Stitch Length: 2.5mm (³⁄₃₂")
Stitch Width: 7mm (⁹⁄₃₂")
Cutting Blade: ON
Decorative Thread: In needle and
upper looper
Foot: Standard

SEAM ALLOWANCE

¼" (6mm)

stepped-up
business card holder

When I first began sewing, I found the flatlock stitch
quite curious. After all, why would I want to make a
stitch where my seams showed?

Wow, has my opinion changed since then! Generally,
I still don't use this stitch for seams when I serge, but I
love it for decorative purposes. And when you thread a
little ribbon through the stitches, it steps the project up
another notch without making it more difficult.

Stepped-Up Project Instructions

1 Randomly mark stitching lines on the Fabric A piece.

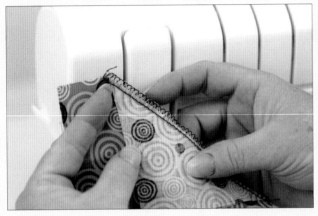

2 Fold Fabric A, right sides together, along a stitching line and flatlock stitch along that line.

3 Open the fold in Fabric A and press flat along the stitching line.

4 Repeat Step 2, flatlock stitching along the remaining lines. Press each stitch open before stitching the next line.

5 Thread the ⅛"-wide (3mm) ribbon through one eye in a double-eyed needle and weave under and over the flatlock stitches.

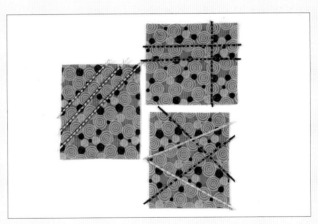

6 Cut a 5" × 6" (13cm × 15cm) rectangle for the business card case from the ribbon-woven Fabric A. Cut out the pockets and lining from Fabrics B and C respectively and assemble the business card case according to the directions on pages 62–63.

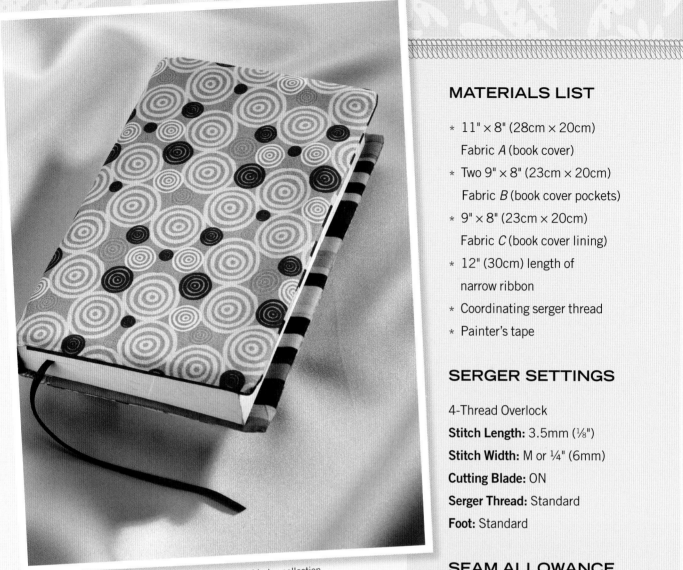

Fabric for this project provided by P&B Textiles from their Linden collection.

MATERIALS LIST

* 11" × 8" (28cm × 20cm)
  Fabric *A* (book cover)
* Two 9" × 8" (23cm × 20cm)
  Fabric *B* (book cover pockets)
* 9" × 8" (23cm × 20cm)
  Fabric *C* (book cover lining)
* 12" (30cm) length of
  narrow ribbon
* Coordinating serger thread
* Painter's tape

SERGER SETTINGS

4-Thread Overlock
Stitch Length: 3.5mm (⅛")
Stitch Width: M or ¼" (6mm)
Cutting Blade: ON
Serger Thread: Standard
Foot: Standard

SEAM ALLOWANCE

¼" (6mm)

book cover

Before my boys could drive, I found myself chauffeuring
them from one activity to the next. While I waited for their
meetings and practices to end, I'd read. Paperback books
were the perfect size to fit into my bag and whip out while
waiting. The problem was, when the book was a romance
novel, the cover pictures made my boys die of embarrass-
ment. A fabric book cover was the perfect solution.

Basic Project Instructions

1 Cut out all fabric pieces as indicated in the Materials List on page 66.

2 Fold the 2 Fabric B pieces in half, wrong sides together, and press.

3 Align a pocket piece to one end of Fabric *A*, right sides together, and serge the pocket to the book cover piece. Repeat for the other pocket piece, aligning it at the opposite end of the book cover fabric.

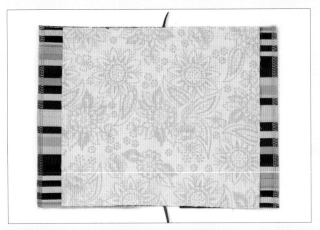

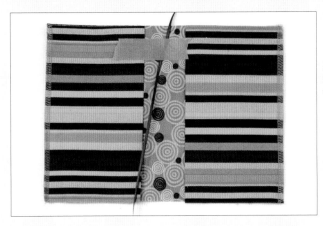

4 Center the ribbon between the pocket pieces on Fabric *A* by aligning the end of the ribbon with the raw edge of the fabric as shown. Use painter's tape to affix.

5 Center Fabric *C* on top of the pockets and the book cover fabric, right sides together, and serge along the top and bottom edges, wrapping the corners as you stitch over the side seams. This will make the corners sharper when the book cover is turned. (See "Wrapping Corners" on page 30.)

6 Turn the lining right side out. Fold both pockets to the lining side of the cover and press all the edges flat. Insert the front and back covers of your book into the fabric pockets.

Fabric for this project provided by P&B Textiles from their Linden collection.

MATERIALS LIST

* 11" × 8" (28cm × 20cm) Fabric *A* (book cover)
* Two 9" × 8" (23cm × 20cm) Fabric *B* (book cover pockets)
* 9" × 8" (23cm × 20cm) Fabric *C* (book cover lining)
* 2 yard (1.8m) length of ⅛" (3mm) narrow ribbon (bookmark)
* Five ½" (13mm) to ¾" (19mm) decorative beads
* Coordinating serger thread
* Decorative thread
* Needle threader large enough for ribbon

SERGER SETTINGS

3-Thread Rolled Edge
Stitch Length: 1.5mm (¹⁄₁₆")
Stitch Width: 3.5mm (⅛")
Cutting Blade: OFF
Serger Thread: Standard, in needle and lower looper
Decorative Thread: In upper looper
Foot: Standard

SEAM ALLOWANCE

¼" (6mm)

stepped-up
book cover

Every reader needs a bookmark. And we all could use a few beads and baubles in our lives. Why not step up our book cover by adding a beautiful beaded bookmark?

You'll have fun selecting beads for this project. Choose shapes, colors and designs that you'll enjoy. The varieties of beads available in craft stores just amaze me. They put the plastic craft beads of my younger days to shame.

Stepped-Up Project Instructions

1 Assemble the book cover according to the instructions and serger settings on pages 66-67.

2 Set up the serger for a rolled edge, with a decorative thread in the upper looper.

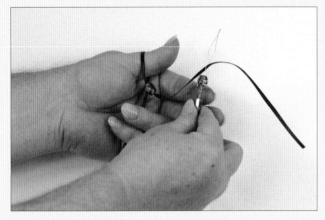

3 Using a needle threader, thread the 5 beads on the narrow ribbon.

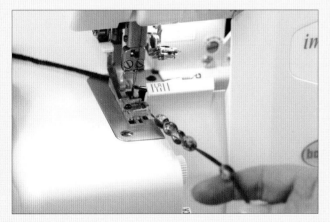

4 Using the rolled hem stitch, serge over approximately 15" (38cm) of the ribbon. Holding the ribbon to the far right will allow the stitch to wrap around it without the ribbon getting caught by the needle.

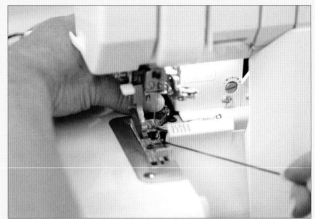

5 Slide a bead behind and to the right of the needle. Stitch about 1" (3cm) beyond the bead, then pull the ribbon to smooth out any excess. Continue to serge, sliding a bead every 6" (15cm). Serge about 15" (38cm) along the ribbon past the last bead.

6 Loop the stitched ribbon so that the beads hang down at the same length. Tie the end of the ribbon around the unbeaded loops, making a tassel with beaded ends.

7 Wrap the end of the ribbon around the unbeaded loops. Use the double-eyed needle to thread the end of the ribbon through the tassel. Place your completed bookmark inside your newly covered book.

Fabric for this project provided by P&B Textiles from their Linden collection.

MATERIALS LIST

* 7¼" × 8" (18cm × 20cm)
  Fabric *A* (checkbook cover)
* Two 7" × 7¼" (17cm × 18cm)
  Fabric *B* (checkbook pockets)
* 7¼" × 7¼" (18cm × 18cm)
  Fabric *C* (checkbook lining)
* 4" (10cm) length of
  ½" (13mm) grosgrain ribbon
* Coordinating serger thread
* Painter's tape

SERGER SETTINGS

4-Thread Overlock
Stitch Length: 3mm (⅛")
Stitch Width: M or ¼" (6mm)
Cutting Blade: ON
Serger Thread: Standard
Foot: Standard

SEAM ALLOWANCE

¼" (6mm)

checkbook cover

Recently, I noticed that a friend of mine had worn out her checkbook. Each time she pulled it out of her purse, she had to remove a rubber band that was holding everything together.

To salvage what was left, I made my friend a beautiful new checkbook cover. You'll have no trouble at all making one for yourself—and since it is both useful and attractive, you'll be glad you did!

Basic Project Instructions

1 Cut out all fabric pieces as indicated in the Materials List on page 70.

2 Cut the ribbon into 2 pieces, each 2" (5cm) long, and fold each piece in half.

3 Mark the center of each 7¼" (18cm) end of Fabric A. Place one piece of folded ribbon on each end, aligning the cut edge of the ribbon with the right side of the center mark. Tape in place.

4 Fold one of the Fabric B pieces in half, wrong sides together, and press. Serge to the 7¼" (18cm) end of the outside edge of Fabric A, stitching the ribbon in place as you serge the pocket to the cover.

5 Serge Fabric C to the remaining 7¼" (18cm) end of Fabric A, right sides together. Stitch the ribbon in place as you serge the lining to the cover.

6 With right sides together, serge the second Fabric B piece together. Turn right side out and press flat.

7 Tuck this pocket piece under the lining close to the seam between the lining and the checkbook cover.

8 Fold the lining on top of the pocket pieces and the checkbook cover, right sides together, and serge along both side seams, wrapping the serged ends as you stitch over them. (The lining will not be as long as the checkbook cover.)

9 Turn the lining right side out and fold both pockets to the lining side of the cover. Press all the edges flat.

71

Fabric for this project provided by P&B Textiles from their Linden collection.

MATERIALS LIST

* 9" × 9" (23cm × 23cm)
  Fabric A (with fused backing)
* Two 7" × 7¼" (17cm × 18cm)
  Fabric B (checkbook pockets)
* 9" × 9" (23cm × 23cm)
  Fabric C (horizontal
  weaving strips)
* 9" × 9" (23cm × 23cm)
  Fabric D (vertical weaving strips)
* 7¼" × 7¼" (18cm × 18cm)
  Fabric E (lining)
* 4" (10cm) length of
  ½" (13mm) grosgrain ribbon
* 9" × 9" (23cm × 23cm)
  fusible web
* Coordinating serger thread
* Decorative thread (2 colors)

SERGER SETTINGS

3-Thread Rolled Edge
Stitch Length: 1.5mm (1⁄16")
Stitch Width: 3.5mm (1⁄8")
Cutting Blade: ON
Serger Thread: Standard, in needle
and lower looper
Decorative Thread: In upper looper
Foot: Standard

SEAM ALLOWANCE

¼" (6mm)

stepped-up
checkbook cover

If you can't decide which fabric to make your checkbook cover out of, pick two and weave them together.
Throw in a decorative thread and your checkbook cover
will be a designer's original, with you as the designer.
This is another impressive technique that is surprising
in its simplicity.

Stepped-Up Project Instructions

1 Iron fusible web to the wrong side of the Fabric *A* square. Set aside.

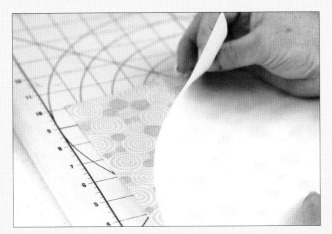

2 Cut the Fabric *C* and Fabric *D* squares into 5 random strips, shaping the strips however you like (straight or curved). Keep the strips in order so you know how they fit back together.

3 With a decorative thread in the upper looper, set the machine to the rolled edge stitch and serge the edges of the horizontal fabric strips.

4 Change the color of the decorative thread in the upper looper, then serge the edges of the vertical fabric strips.

5 Lay the horizontal strips, in order, on the fusible web side of the Fabric *A* square. Weave the vertical strips with the horizontal strips.

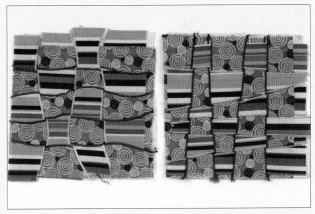

6 When all the strips have been woven together, fuse them to the Fabric *A* square. From this, cut a 7¼" × 8" (18cm × 20cm) rectangle for the checkbook cover.

7 Assemble the checkbook cover according to the directions and serger settings on pages 70–71.

Fabric for this project provided by P&B Textiles from their Linden collection.

MATERIALS LIST

* 20" × 9½" (51cm × 24cm) Fabric A (gift bag)
* Two 2¼" × 8½" (6cm × 22cm) Fabric B (casings)
* 8" × 18½" (20cm × 47cm) Fabric C (band)
* 2 yard (1.8m) length of ¼" (6mm) ribbon
* Coordinating serger thread

SERGER SETTINGS

4-Thread Overlock
Stitch Length: 3mm (⅛")
Stitch Width: M or ¼" (6mm)
Cutting Blade: ON
Serger Thread: Standard
Foot: Standard

SEAM ALLOWANCE

¼" (6mm)

gift bag

At Christmas my family gives stocking stuffers, each person buying a $2 to $3 gift for everyone else. One year my oldest son worked in a grocery store and did his shopping at work—and bought his grandma a 10-pound bag of potatoes and some packets of gravy mix. Have you ever tried to wrap a bag of potatoes? That was the year I first made gift bags. They're so easy, you'll want to make co-ordinated bags for all your gifts.

Basic Project Instructions

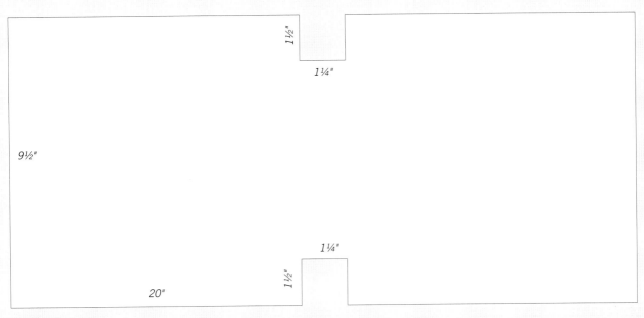

Gift Bag Template
Enlarge by 296%.

1½"

1¼"

9½"

1¼"

1½"

20"

1 Cut 1½" × 1¼" (38mm × 32mm) rectangles in Fabric *A* as indicated in the template above.

2 Finish the ends of both Fabric *B* pieces by serging each 2¼" (6cm) end separately. Press the serged ends to the wrong side of the casing.

3 Fold the casing pieces in half lengthwise, wrong sides together, and press. Set the casing pieces aside.

4 Serge the 8" (20cm) ends of Fabric *C*, right sides together. Fold the band in half lengthwise, wrong sides together, and press. Set the band aside.

5 Mark the center bottom on Fabric *A* by folding the bag in half and pressing flat, creating a crease along the center bottom between the rectangular cutout areas.

8 Pin the folded casings to the bag, centering each casing between the side seams, one on the front and one on the back. (If you feel comfortable putting these elements together without pins, please do!)

6 Fold the bag in half, right sides together, and serge both side seams. Press the seams to one side.

9 Pin the folded band to the casing/bag pieces, aligning the seam with one of the side seams.

7 Create the boxed bottom by folding one side seam to the center bottom mark and serge along the raw edges.

Repeat on the second side seam. Turn the bag right side out.

10 Serge along the raw edges of the bag, casing and band. Take care to remove the pins before the cutting blade reaches them. Fold the band and casing upward and press flat.

11 Cut the ribbon into two 1-yard (91cm) pieces.

12 Starting on a side seam, thread one of the ribbons through both casings and tie the ends together. Repeat on the opposite side seam.

13 You may put a 3½" × 5½" (9cm × 14cm) piece of cardboard in the bottom of the bag for added stability.

Fabric for this project provided by P&B Textiles from their Linden collection.

stepped-up
gift bag

You can't have a properly wrapped present without a pretty bow. And for the beautiful gift bag you have made, you need a very pretty bow indeed! You can choose to step it up with a wired ribbon bow or a dainty rosette. Either way, your present is sure to be the prettiest at the party.

MATERIALS LIST

* 20" × 9½" (51cm × 24cm)
  Fabric A (bag)
* Two 2¼" × 8½" (6cm × 22cm)
  Fabric B (casings)
* 8" × 18½" (20cm × 47cm)
  Fabric C (band)
* 3" × 44" (8cm × 112cm)
  Fabric D (bow)
* 3" × 44" (8cm × 112cm)
  Fabric E (rosette)
* 2 yard (1.8m) length of
  ¼" (6mm) ribbon
* Coordinating serger thread
* Decorative thread
* 24-gauge craft wire

SERGER SETTINGS

Settings vary in Steps 3, 8, 10.

4-Thread Overlock
Stitch Length: 3mm (⅛")
Stitch Width: M or ¼" (6mm)
Cutting Blade: ON
Serger Thread: Standard
Foot: Standard

SEAM ALLOWANCE

¼" (6mm)

Stepped-Up Project Instructions

1 Create the gift bag by following the directions on pages 74–77.

2 Cut the fabric for the bow and the rosette out of Fabric *D* and Fabric *E* (see template on page 80).

SERGER SETTINGS
(STEP 3)

3-Thread Rolled Edge
Stitch Length: 1.5mm (1/16")
Stitch Width: 3.5mm (1/8")
Cutting Blade: OFF
Serger Thread: Standard, in needle and lower looper
Decorative Thread: In upper looper
Foot: Foot with wire guides

3 Thread the wire through the guides in the foot. Turn the cutting blade off.

4 Using the rolled edge stitch, serge over the wire along both edges of the bow.

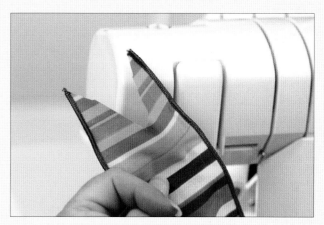

5 Apply a small amount of seam sealant to the ends of the rolled edges. When the seam sealant has dried, cut a *V* in the ends of the bow.

Fold

Template for Rosette
Enlarge 280%.

6 Tie the bow and pin to the gift bag.

7 To make the rosette, taper the ends of the rosette fabric as indicated by the template above. This taper does not have to be exact; you just want both ends to come to a point.

SERGER SETTINGS
(STEP 8)

3-Thread Rolled Edge
Stitch Length: 1.5mm (1/16")
Stitch Width: 3.5mm (1/8")
Cutting Blade: ON
Serger Thread: Standard, in needle and lower looper
Decorative Thread: In upper looper
Foot: Standard

8 Set the serger for the rolled edge stitch with the decorative thread in the upper looper. Place the standard foot on the serger and turn off the cutting blade.

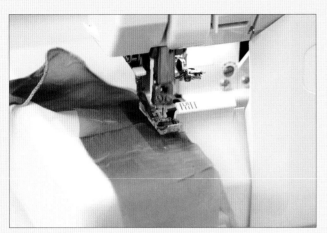

9 Using the rolled edge stitch, serge along one edge of the rosette fabric.

10 Serge along the cut edge opposite the rolled edge. This will add some gathers to the fabric.

SERGER SETTINGS
(STEP 10)

4-Thread Overlock

Stitch Length: 4mm (5/32")

Stitch Width: M or ¼" (6mm)

Cutting Blade: ON

Serger Thread: Standard

Differential Feed: 2

Foot: Standard

11 Pull a needle thread to gather the rosette fabric as tightly as possible, rolling the fabric into a rosette shape. With needle and thread, sew through all the layers of the rosette, gathering it into a rose shape.

12 Pin the rosette to your gift bag.

Serging Into The Curves

Oftentimes the old cliché rings true: Just when you think you have everything figured out, life throws you a curveball. Serging is no different. Just when you think you've learned all the necessary techniques to be a master serger, the projects in this chapter throw you a few curves. But don't be nervous, fellow sergers; if you can handle straight line stitching and fabric layering, I know you can handle curves.

By applying the skills you learned in the previous chapters and combining them with a few curved stitches, you will create these functional and beautiful projects in a matter of minutes. Before you know it, you'll be an expert serger who's able to serge anything that is thrown your way.

Fabric for this project provided by P&B Textiles from their Linden collection.

MATERIALS LIST

* ¼ yard (23cm) Fabric *A* (pot holder)
* ¼ yard (23cm) Fabric *B* (pot holder pockets)
* ¼ yard (23cm) Fabric *C* (pot holder lining)
* 3" (8cm) length of ¼" (6mm) ribbon
* 9" × 9" (23cm ×23cm) heat-resistant batting for making pot holders (such as Insul-Brite)
* Coordinating serger thread
* Painter's tape

SERGER SETTINGS

4-Thread Overlock
Stitch Length: 3mm (⅛")
Stitch Width: M or ¼" (6mm)
Cutting Blade: ON
Serger Thread: Standard
Foot: Standard

SEAM ALLOWANCE

¼" (6mm)

pot holder

Over the years, my Granny Ree must have made thousands of pot holders, using any and all scraps of fabric available to craft them. Anyone who ever visited her house left with at least one or two of her pot holders.

Granny Ree is gone, but her pot holder legacy lives on in kitchens across Oklahoma, Missouri and Arkansas. To honor that legacy, I'm going teach you to make pot holders, too. You might even want to make them for all *your* guests.

Basic Project Instructions

Pot Holder, Batting and Lining Template
Enlarge 308%.

1 Photocopy the templates (above and on page 87) for the pot holder and pockets (enlarge as indicated). Cut out and mark all the fabric pieces.

2 Lay the pot holder Fabric *A*, wrong side down, on top of the heat-resistant batting.

3 Fold the pocket pieces in half, wrong sides together, and press flat.

4 Place the pocket pieces on top of the pot holder fabric, right sides together.

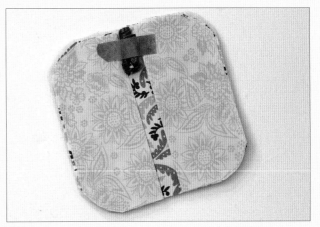

5 Fold the ribbon in half and tape between the pockets, centered on one side of the fabric and batting, aligning the ends of the ribbon with the edge of the fabric.

6 Place the lining on top of the pockets and ribbon, right sides together, matching the placement marks. The lining will not completely cover one of the pockets. Serge around the outside edges of the pot holder.

7 Turn the pot holder by folding the lining right side out and folding the pockets to the back. Press the seams flat.

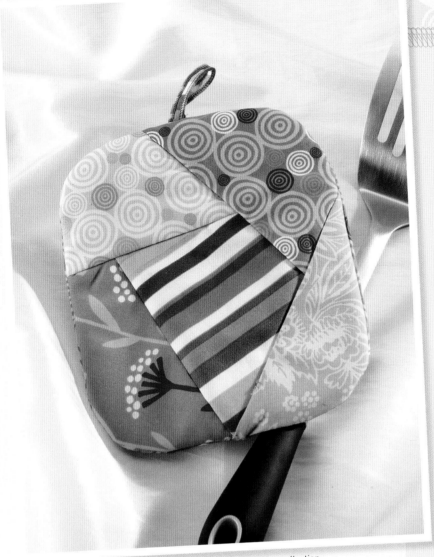

Fabric for this project provided by P&B Textiles from their Linden collection.

MATERIALS LIST

* 5 fabric scraps, 3½" × 7"
  (9cm × 18cm) each
  (crazy patch pot holder front)
* ¼ yard (23cm) Fabric *B*
  (pot holder pockets)
* ¼ yard (23cm) Fabric *C*
  (for pot holder lining)
* 3" (8cm) length of
  ¼" (6mm) ribbon
* 9" × 9" (23cm × 23cm) heat-
  resistant batting for making pot
  holders (such as Insul-Brite)
* Coordinating serger thread

SERGER SETTINGS

4-Thread Overlock
Stitch Length: 3mm (⅛")
Stitch Width: M or ¼" (6mm)
Cutting Blade: ON
Serger Thread: Standard
Foot: Standard

SEAM ALLOWANCE

¼" (6mm)

stepped-up
pot holder

The first quilt I ever made was a crazy patch quilt. I was
about 12 years old at the time, and I didn't even know
the technique had a name. I just knew that I wanted
to make a quilt and was limited to the fabric I had.

We all need to get a little crazy from time to time,
so why not give it a try with this stepped-up pot holder?
There just may be a crazy patch quilt in your future.

Stepped-Up Project Instructions

Cut 2 of Fabric B

Pot Holder Pockets Template
Enlarge 308%.

1 Serge 2 of the fabric scraps, right sides together, and press the seam to one side.

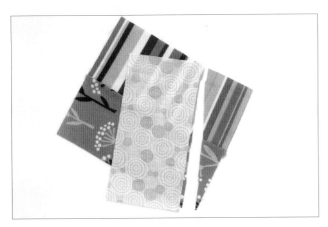

2 Lay another fabric scrap on top of the panel and trim the uneven edges of the panel to match up with the new scrap. Serge along this straight edge and press the seam to one side.

3 Repeat Step 2, layering fabrics, trimming uneven edges and serging along the straight edge until all your fabric scraps have been added.

4 Cut the front of the pot holder from the crazy patch panel.

5 Cut out and mark the remaining fabric pieces as instructed on pages 84–85; follow the instructions there to assemble and complete the pot holder.

Fabric for this project provided by P&B Textiles from their Linden collection.

MATERIALS LIST

* ¼ yard (23cm) Fabric *A* (stocking)
* ¼ yard (23cm) Fabric *B* (stocking lining)
* ¼ yard (23cm) Fabric *C* (stocking band)
* 5" (13cm) length of ½" (13mm) ribbon
* Painter's tape
* Coordinating serger thread

SERGER SETTINGS

4-Thread Overlock
Stitch Length: 3mm (⅛")
Stitch Width: M or ¼" (6mm)
Cutting Blade: ON
Serger Thread: Standard
Foot: Standard

SEAM ALLOWANCE

¼" (6mm)

christmas stocking

I love to make stockings! Over the years I have made hundreds, whether sewing them for my charity group, for all the grandchildren at my Grandma's Christmas celebration or for the children in my sons' classes at school. When I taught, this was one of my favorite projects for students.

When you see how easy these stockings are to make, you just might try to beat my stocking-making record!

Basic Project Instructions

1 Photocopy the templates on page 91 (enlarge as indicated). Cut 2 stocking pieces from Fabric *A*, 2 lining pieces from Fabric *B* and 1 stocking band from Fabric *C*.

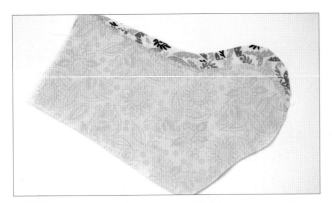

2 Layer the lining pieces, right sides together, and the stocking pieces, right sides together, then serge around the foot portion of the stocking.

3 Turn the lining pieces to the outside.

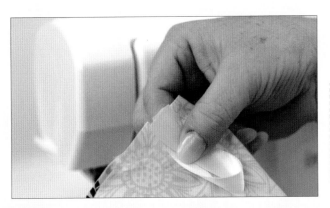

4 Fold the ribbon in half and tape to the top of the stocking, aligning the ribbon to the heel side seam. The ends of the ribbon should be aligned with the edge of the fabric and placed next to the lining fabric. Set aside.

5 Create the band by folding the band piece in half, right sides together, then serging a 7" (18cm) side seam.

Fold the band in half lengthwise, wrong sides together, and press flat.

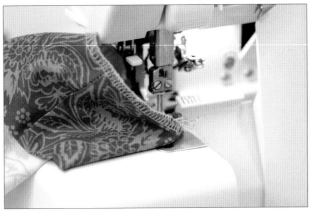

6 Place the band around the top of the stocking, with the band fabric next to the lining fabric. Align the band side seam with the heel side seam and serge together through all layers.

7 Turn the stocking right side out and fold the band down. Press to smooth all the seams.

Mastering the Circular Motion

When serging around a narrow circular area, you will find it easier to serge with the foot inside the circle.

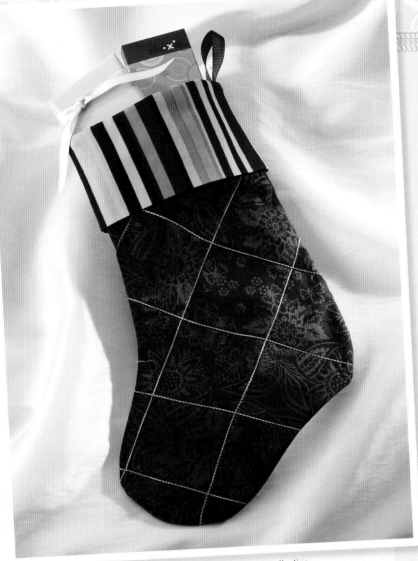

Fabric for this project provided by P&B Textiles from their Linden collection.

stepped-up
christmas stocking

We all have different tastes in holiday decorations. Sometimes a shopping trip for the perfect stocking fabric yields less than desirable results. Even suitable fabric can leave you feeling that something's missing: details, frills or perhaps a little more texture to achieve that perfect look.

This stepped-up version shows that something as simple as a chain stitch with decorative thread can add that special touch you're looking for.

MATERIALS LIST

* ¼ yard (23cm) Fabric *A* (stocking)
* ¼ yard (23cm) Fabric *B* (stocking lining)
* ¼ yard (23cm) Fabric *C* (stocking band)
* 5" (13cm) length of ½" (13mm) ribbon
* Coordinating serger thread
* Decorative thread
* Painter's tape

SERGER SETTINGS

Chain Stitch
Stitch Length: 3mm (⅛")
Stitch Width: M or ¼" (6mm)
Cutting Blade: OFF
Serger Thread: Standard, in needle
Decorative Thread: In chain looper
Foot: Standard

SEAM ALLOWANCE

¼" (6mm)

Stepped-Up Project Instructions

*Cut 1 from Fabric C
and place on fold*

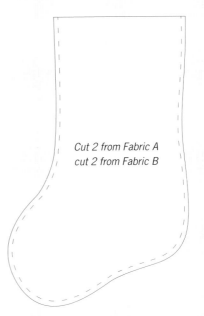

*Cut 2 from Fabric A
cut 2 from Fabric B*

Stocking Band Template
For both basic and stepped-up stockings. Enlarge 229%.

Stocking Template
For both basic and stepped-up stockings. Enlarge 452%.

1 Photocopy the templates above (enlarge as indicated). Cut out and mark all pattern pieces.

3 Assemble the stocking according to the directions on pages 88–89.

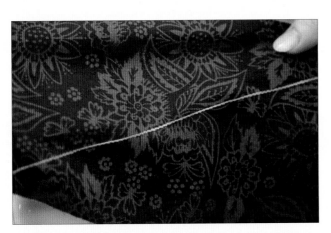

2 Using the chain stitch, with the wrong side of the fabric up, stitch along the grid lines. When the fabric is turned over, the decorative loops of the chain will be on the right side of the fabric.

Fabric for this project provided by P&B Textiles from their Linden collection.

MATERIALS LIST

* 8" x 8" (20cm × 20cm)
  Fabric *A* (glasses case)
* 8" x 8" (20cm × 20cm)
  Fabric *B* (glasses case lining)
* 8" x 8" (20cm × 20cm) batting
* Coordinating serger thread

SERGER SETTINGS

4-Thread Overlock
Stitch Length: 3mm (⅛")
Stitch Width: M or ¼" (6mm)
Cutting Blade: ON
Serger Thread: Standard
Foot: Standard

SEAM ALLOWANCE

¼" (6mm)

glasses case

The glasses case is one of my favorite gift projects. I knew it was a hit when I made one for a friend using fabric with her favorite college football team's logo. Next day after the big game, she called to request more glasses cases for her game-time friends.

The moral of the story: Be prepared! These cases are so great, you never know when a gift might lead to a request for more.

Basic Project Instructions

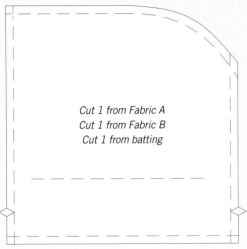

Glasses Case Template
Enlarge 301%.

Cut 1 from Fabric A
Cut 1 from Fabric B
Cut 1 from batting

1 Photocopy the glasses case template above (enlarge as indicated). Cut out and mark all fabric pieces.

2 Layer the lining and glasses case fabric, right sides together, on top of the batting. (Place the wrong side of the lining next to the batting.)

3 Serge along the top, curved edge. Press the seam toward the lining.

4 Fold the glasses case Fabric *A*, right sides together, matching the notches, then fold the lining and batting (right sides of the lining together), matching the notches.

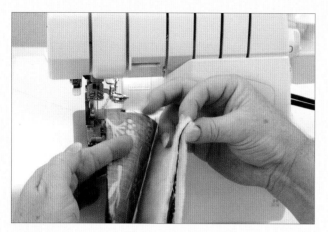

5 Fold the layers of the lining and Fabric *A* together, matching up all the pieces at the notches. Serge through all layers along the notched side seam.

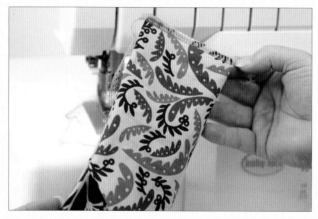

6 Turn the lining to the outside and serge through all layers along the bottom.

7 Turn right side out and press seams flat.

MATERIALS LIST

* 8" × 8" (20cm × 20cm)
  Fabric A (glasses case)

* 8" × 8" (20cm × 20cm)
  Fabric B (glasses case lining)

* 2" × 18" (5cm × 46cm)
  Fabric C (piping)

* 18" (46cm) length of
  3/16" (5mm) narrow cording

* 8" × 8" (20cm × 20cm) batting

* Coordinating serger thread

* Cording foot

SERGER SETTINGS

4-Thread Overlock

Stitch Length: 3mm (1/8")

Stitch Width: M or 1/4" (6mm)

Cutting Blade: ON

Serger Thread: Standard

Foot: Cording

SEAM ALLOWANCE

1/4" (6mm)

Fabric for this project provided by P&B Textiles from their Linden collection.

stepped-up
glasses case

Nothing makes a project look more tailored than piping, and adding piping is a great way to step up your serging skills. When shopping, though, you'll find that piping color options are limited. That's why I make my own piping.

There's no easier way to do it than on the serger. All you need is a cording foot, some cording and a fabric strip. Master this technique and you're sure to add piping to a number of your favorite projects!

Stepped-Up Project Instructions

1 Photocopy template on page 93 (enlarge as indicated). Cut out and mark all pattern pieces.

2 Attach the cording foot to the serger.

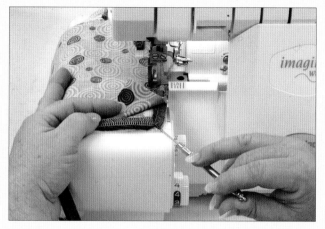

3 Fold the piping fabric around the cording and place under the cording foot, with the cording in the groove in the foot. Create the piping by serging the length of the fabric.

5 Fold the piping around the corner and lay in place along the notched edge of the outside fabric. The piping will turn the corner easier if you make a 45° cut in the piping seam allowance before you stitch off the end.

6 Fold the outside, right sides together, matching the notches, and fold the lining and batting, right sides of the lining together, matching the notches. The piping will be between the layers of the outside fabric.

4 Place the piping between the outside fabric and the lining, along the curved edge. Serge along the curved seam, between the dots.

7 Fold the layers of the lining and outside fabric together, matching up all the pieces at the notches.

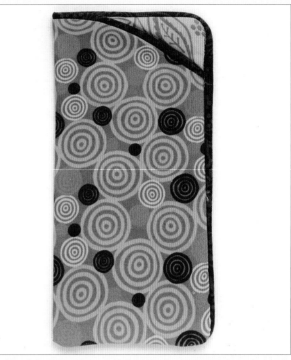

10 Turn right side out and press seams flat.

8 Place the piping under the groove in the cording foot and serge through all layers along the notched side seam.

9 Turn the lining to the outside and serge through all layers along the bottom.

Fabric for this project provided by P&B Textiles from their Linden collection.

MATERIALS LIST

* ¼ yard (23cm) Fabric *A* (back flap)
* ¼ yard (23cm) Fabric *B* (right flap)
* ¼ yard (23cm) Fabric *C* (left flap)
* ¼ yard (23cm) Fabric *D* (pocket)
* 1 yard (91cm) length of cording
* Coordinating serger thread
* Painter's tape
* Seam sealant

SERGER SETTINGS

4-Thread Overlock
Stitch Length: 3mm (⅛")
Stitch Width: M or ¼" (6mm)
Cutting Blade: ON
Serger Thread: Standard
Foot: Standard

SEAM ALLOWANCE

¼" (6mm)

neck purse

I hate to drag around my purse at sewing events or quilt shows. Generally I carry a large bag to hold my new treasures, but my money, phone and keys would get lost amid all the items I pick up.

The neck purse is perfect for all of those essentials we need to get to quickly. I'm sure there are times when you'd rather leave the big purse at home. Those are the times when the neck purse is just what you need!

Basic Project Instructions

1 Photocopy the templates on page 101 (enlarge as indicated). Cut out and mark all the pattern pieces.

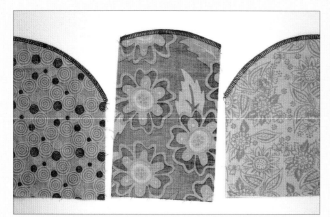

2 Serge the curved edges of the back flap (above center), right sides together.

Serge the curved edges of the left flap (above left) and right flap (above right), right sides together.

3 Turn the right flap and left flap right side out and press the seams flat.

4 Fold the pocket in half, wrong sides together, and press flat.

5 Lay the back flap on the work surface with the right side of the fabric facing up.

6 Align the left flap on the left side of the back flap (top center, above), right sides together; the curve of the left flap should be next to the seam at the curve of the back flap.

Align the right flap to the right side of the back flap (bottom center, above) just as you did the left flap.

Layer the pocket on top of all flap pieces (left, above), lining up the straight edge at the bottom of the bag.

7 Tape the cording in place on both sides of the bag. The cut end of the cording should extend about 2" (5cm) past the raw edge of the fabric.

8 Fold the other section of the back flap over all the other elements. Wrap the loose ends of the cording around the back flap and tape in place.

9 Serge both of the side seams. As you come to the ends of the cording, fold them back over the fabric, taping the ends in place.

Be sure that you don't cut the tails off; rather, simply serge over them. This means you'll need to turn off the cutting blade before you stitch past the cording. If turning off the blade is not a simple twist of the knob on your serger, carefully guide the ribbons next to the cutting blade to prevent the cording from being cut.

10 Trim off the excess tails of the cording, Apply seam sealant to the cording in the serged seam area.

Creating the Cording

If you find several colors of cording that match your fabrics and you just can't decide which one to use, use them all! For this project, I braided multiple strands and tied the cords together every few inches.

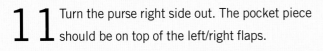

11 Turn the purse right side out. The pocket piece should be on top of the left/right flaps.

12 Serge along the bottom edge of the bag, through all of the layers.

13 Fold the pocket to the opposite side of the bag, enclosing the bottom seam in the pocket.

The flap pieces will fold down over the pocket when it is worn around the neck.

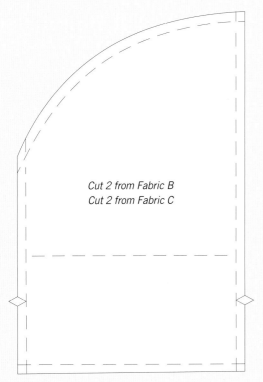

Cut 2 from Fabric B
Cut 2 from Fabric C

Neck Purse Side Flap Template
Enlarge 265%.

Cutting line for pocket

Pocket
Cut 1 from Fabric D

Back Flap
Cut 2 from Fabric A

Neck Purse Back Flap and Pocket Template
Enlarge 202%.

Fabric for this project provided by P&B Textiles from their Linden collection.

* ¼ yard (23cm) Fabric *A* (back flap)
* ¼ yard (23cm) Fabric *B* (right flap)
* ¼ yard (23cm) Fabric *C* (left flap)
* ¼ yard (23cm) Fabric *D* (pocket)
* 1 yard (91cm) length of cording
* 2–3 decorative threads
* Coordinating serger thread
* Painter's tape
* Stretch nylon thread (such as Wooly Nylon)
* Seam sealant

SERGER SETTINGS

Settings vary in Step 6.

3-Thread Rolled Edge
Stitch Length: 1.5mm (¹⁄₁₆")
Stitch Width: ⅛" (3.5mm)
Cutting Blade: ON
Serger Thread: Standard, in needle
Decorative Thread: In upper looper
Stretch Nylon Thread: In lower looper
Foot: Standard

SEAM ALLOWANCE

¼" (6mm)

stepped-up
neck purse

When I was a child, my mom tried everything to get my hair to curl. Stinky perms, pink sponge rollers, even bobby pin curls—nothing worked. No matter what she tried, we couldn't get the cute little ringlets that she was hoping for.

Now that I'm all grown up, I can have perfect ringlets any day I want—thanks to my serger! As you'll see, these curls are the easiest you'll ever make. (They add a nice decorative touch to your neck purse, too.)

Stepped-Up Project Instructions

1 Photocopy the templates on page 101 (enlarge as indicated). Cut out and mark all the fabric pieces.

2 Set the machine for a rolled edge stitch with a decorative thread in the upper looper and stretch nylon thread in the lower looper. The upper looper thread will be the dominant color of the curls.

3 Tighten the tension on the lower looper. If you have a serger with automatic tensions, you will have to manually tighten the lower looper thread by holding the thread tightly between your fingers as you serge.

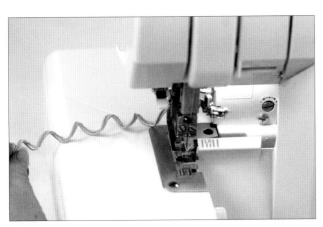

4 As you stitch, the thread chain will curl. If your chain is not curling, your lower looper tension is not tight enough. You want a total of 5 curls each, about 4–5" (10cm–13cm) long when curled. Your curls can all be the same color, or you can change the color of the upper looper thread for a different color curl.

5 Apply seam sealant on both ends of the curls. Tape the curls in place on the back flap, with the ends of the curls slightly extended past the end of the fabric.

SERGER SETTINGS
(STEP 6)

4-Thread Overlock
Stitch Length: 3mm (⅛")
Stitch Width: M or ¼" (6mm)
Cutting Blade: ON
Serger Thread: Standard
Foot: Standard

6 With right sides together, serge the back flap pieces together along the curved edge. Fold the tails of the curls back over the raw edge of the fabric before you serge across the curls.

7 Cut off the excess tails of the curls. Apply sealant to the curls in the serged seam area. Assemble the remainder of the bag according to the directions on pages 98–101.

Remaking the Ready-Made

My high school home economics teacher challenged my love of sewing in so many wonderful ways. One of the many lessons to stay with me over the years was how to remake an item into something totally different, yet still functional. I always look forward to such a challenge, and I know you will, too.

If you think alterations involve only hemming, you're in for a real treat. In this chapter, you'll discover that by altering existing ready-made pieces, you can create a wide variety of useful items. In the following projects, you will alter towels, hand towels and fingertip towels, turning them into household essentials that you will love using and giving as gifts. So sit back, relax and enjoy remaking the ready-made.

MATERIALS LIST

* Lightweight bath towel (hair wrap)
* 1½" × 12" (4cm × 30cm) Fabric *A* (hair wrap loop)
* 6" (15cm) length of ⅜" (1cm) elastic
* Coordinating serger thread

SERGER SETTINGS

4-Thread Overlock
Stitch Length: 3mm (⅛")
Stitch Width: M or ¼" (6mm)
Cutting Blade: ON
Serger Thread: Standard
Foot: Standard

SEAM ALLOWANCE

¼" (6mm)

hair wrap

I've sponsored overnight school and church events over the years, and I've always been amazed at the towels that girls go through (two per shower—one for the body, one for the head). I wondered how moms with daughters ever keep up with the laundry.

I created this project for those mothers (and their girls), but it's a great graduation gift as well. One towel makes two hair wraps, so keep one wrap for yourself!

Basic Project Instructions

Cut 2 from bath towel

Hair Wrap Template
Enlarge by 430%.

Cut 1 from Fabric A and place on fold

Hair Wrap Loop Template
Enlarge by 135%.

1 Photocopy the hair wrap template and the loop template above (enlarge as indicated). The curves are general sizes—you don't need to worry about getting the perfect shape. Cut 2 hair wrap pieces from the bath towel and 1 loop piece from Fabric *A* for each towel wrap.

2 Fold the loop piece in half lengthwise, right sides together, and serge along the side seam. Turn right side out and press.

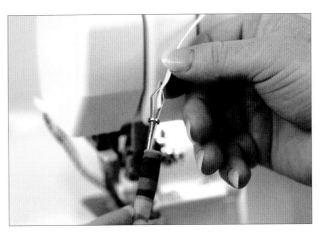

3 Thread the elastic through the loop.

6 To finish the cut edge opening of the hair wrap, start at the back seam and serge through a single layer all around the opening.

How to Use the Hair Wrap

Arrange the larger curved portion around your head. Twist the narrow portion at your forehead. When the wrap feels snug, fold the tail back and tuck it into the elastic loop.

4 Serge the elastic loop to the right side of one of the towel pieces, approximately 12" (30cm) from the bottom of the back. (The back is the large curved end.) The raw edges of the loop should be lined up with the cut edge of the towel.

5 Serge the hair wrap pieces, right sides together, along the curved edge.

MATERIALS LIST

* Lightweight bath towel
  (hair wrap)
* 3" × 35" (8cm × 89cm)
  Fabric A (hair wrap band)
* 20" (51cm) length of
  1" (3cm) elastic
* Coordinating serger thread

SERGER SETTINGS

4-Thread Overlock

Stitch Length: 3mm (⅛")

Stitch Width: M or ¼" (6mm)

Cutting Blade: ON

Serger Thread: Standard

Foot: Standard

SEAM ALLOWANCE

¼" (6mm)

Fabric for this project provided by P&B Textiles from their Linden collection.

stepped-up
hair wrap

Using your serger to put in an elastic casing gives the seams of your project a finished look. This hair wrap is perfect for practicing stretching the elastic as you serge. If the cap is a little fuller in one place or another, the hair wrap will still fit, so have fun and get comfortable with this technique. Soon you'll be ready to take on other projects with elastic casings.

Stepped-Up Project Instructions

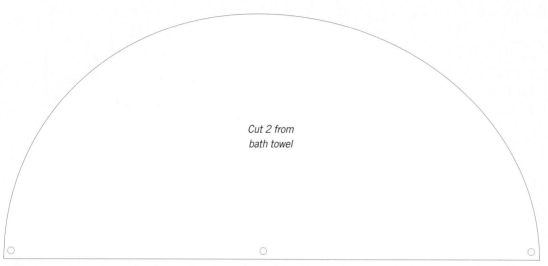

Stepped-Up Hair Wrap Template
Enlarge by 306%.

Cut 2 from bath towel

1 Photocopy the stepped-up hair wrap template above (enlarge as indicated). The curves are general sizes—you don't need to worry about getting the perfect shape. Cut 2 hair wrap pieces from the bath towel. The 3" × 25" (8cm × 64cm) piece of Fabric *A* is your hair wrap band.

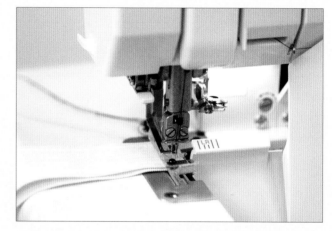

2 Serge the hair wrap pieces, right sides together, along the curved edge.

3 Serge the ends of the band, right sides together, creating a ring. Press the band in half lengthwise, wrong sides together. Make quarter placement marks around the band every 8½" (22cm), starting at the seam.

4 Serge the ends of the elastic together. Make quarter placement marks around the elastic every 5" (13cm), starting at the seam.

5 Tuck the elastic into the fold of the band and pin at the placement marks.

6 Pin the band to the cap at the placement marks.

7 Serge the band to the cap, taking care to remove the pins before serging a pinned area. Turn the cap right side out.

Removing the Pins

I rarely use pins with my serger. Serging over a pin can cause damage to your machine, resulting in a trip to the repair shop. However, when working with elastic, I find it easiest to use pins. Take extra care to remove them as you stitch.

MATERIALS LIST

* Hand towel (hood)
* Bath towel (body of hooded towel)
* Coordinating serger thread

SERGER SETTINGS

4-Thread Overlock
Stitch Length: 3mm (⅛")
Stitch Width: M or ¼" (6mm)
Cutting Blade: ON
Foot: Standard

SEAM ALLOWANCE

¼" (6mm)

hooded towel

In the summer, my family spends a lot of time at the pool. It amazes me how quickly the little ones take to the water and how long they want to stay in. It's also amazing how quickly they get chilled when they get back out.

This hooded towel is guaranteed to keep little swimmers covered from head to toe while they dry off. It comes in handy at bath time (and goes perfectly with the bath mitt on page 116).

Basic Project Instructions

1 Cut the hand towel in half lengthwise. (You'll need only one half.)

2 To create the hood, fold one half piece of the hand towel in half, right sides together, and serge along the cut edge.

3 Fold the bath towel in half to find the center of one edge, then mark the center.

4 Align the hood with the towel, right sides together, matching up the seam of the hood to the center mark on the towel.

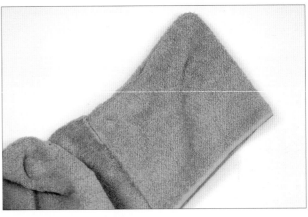

5 Serge the hood to the towel. Use a double-eyed needle to run the serger tail under the serger stitches.

Getting Specific About Stopping and Starting

On most serger seams, you can simply start serging, then feed your fabric under the foot. However, in some instances it's important to start and stop the serged seam at a specific point. Joining the hood to the towel is one of those times.

To do this, raise the needles and presser foot and align the starting point under the needle area; lower the needles and presser foot and being to serge.

MATERIALS LIST

* Hand towel (hood)
* Bath towel (body of hooded towel)
* 1½ yard (1.4m) length of bias tape
* Coordinating serger thread

SERGER SETTINGS

Wide Cover Stitch

Stitch Length: 3mm (⅛")
Stitch Width: M or ¼" (6mm)
Cutting Blade: OFF
Serger Thread: Standard
Foot: Standard

SEAM ALLOWANCE

¼" (6mm)

stepped-up
hooded towel

Perhaps you love the idea of making hooded towels for yourself or as gifts but feel they lack decorative pizzazz. Just spruce them up by adding bias trim to the hoods.

The wide cover stitch is ideal for this: The two needles stitch down the outer edges of the trim, creating perfectly spaced rows. When you see how easy it is to add trim to the hood, you may want to embellish the body of your towel, too.

Stepped-Up Project Instructions

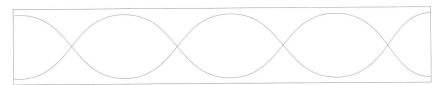

Stepped-Up Hooded Towel Trim Template Enlarge 380%.

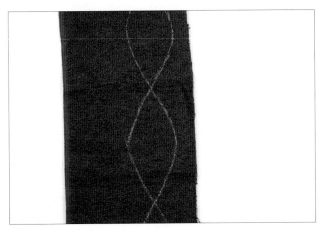

1 Cut the hand towel in half lengthwise. Photocopy the trim template above (enlarge as indicated). Using only one of the half pieces of the hand towel, mark placement lines using the template.

3 Assemble the hooded towel according to the instructions on pages 112–113.

2 Place the bias tape right side up along both placement lines. With the wide cover stitch, attach the bias tape to the hand towel.

MATERIALS LIST

* Hand towel (bath mitt)
* Coordinating serger thread

SERGER SETTINGS

Thread Overlock
Stitch Length: 3mm (⅛")
Stitch Width: M or ¼" (6mm)
Cutting Blade: ON
Serger Thread: Standard
Foot: Standard

SEAM ALLOWANCE

¼" (6mm)

bath mitt

If you've ever bathed a baby, you know how hard it is to handle the wiggling and squirming with a washcloth.

Bath mitts were virtually unheard of when my boys were babies. Even today, bath mitts tend to be primarily decorative. So why not make your own?

Combine this bath mitt with the hooded towel for a perfect gift for new parents. The bath mitt is also great for washing your car or cleaning up a spill.

Basic Project Instructions

1 Photocopy the bath mitt template on this page (enlarge as indicated). Cut 2 bath mitt pieces from the hand towel.

2 With right sides together, serge around the bath mitt pieces.

3 Finish the opening of the bath mitt by serging around the bottom edge. (Serging will be easier if you position the bath mitt around the presser foot.)

4 Turn the bath mitt right side out.

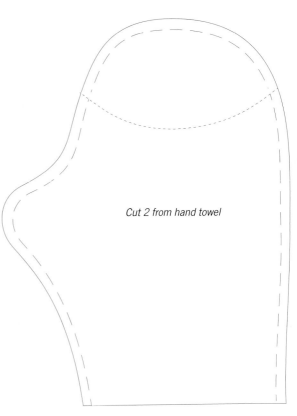

Cut 2 from hand towel

Bath Mitt Template
Enlarge 233%.

MATERIALS LIST

* Hand towel (bath mitt)
* ½ yard (46cm) length of bias strip (width appropriate for bias binding accessory)
* 8" (20cm) length of bias tape
* Bias binding accessory
* Coordinating serger thread
* Spray starch

SERGER SETTINGS

Settings vary in Steps 5 and 7.

Wide Cover Stitch
Stitch Length: 3mm (⅛")
Stitch Width: M or ¼" (6mm)
Cutting Blade: OFF
Serger Thread: Standard
Foot: Standard

SEAM ALLOWANCE

¼" (6mm)

stepped-up
bath mitt

Many sergers with the cover stitch capability have a double-fold bias binder accessory available. This binding will allow you to put a finished edge to the cuff of the bath mitt, similar to the binding on a quilt. And the best part: All of the raw edges are folded and stitched with little-to-no effort from you.

Stepped-Up Project Instructions

1 Photocopy the bath mitt template on page 117 (enlarge as indicated). Cut the bath mitt pieces from the hand towel and mark according to the template.

2 With right sides together, attach the bath mitt pieces by serging a 5" (15cm) seam along the straight edge of the bath mitts (the side opposite the thumb, from the wrist up 5" [15cm]).

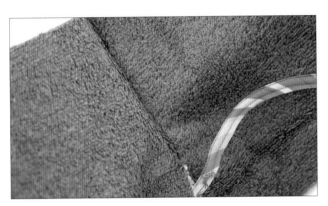

3 Place the bias tape right side up on the placement line and stitch in place with the wide cover stitch.

4 Heavily starch the bias strip until it's stiff.

5 Insert the starched bias strip in the bias binder accessory. Attach the binding to the bottom of the bath mitt, extending the tail of the binding about 1" (25mm) past the end of the mitt.

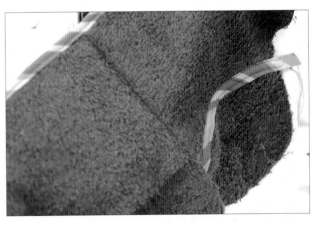

SERGER SETTINGS
(STEP 5)

Chain Stitch
Stitch Length: 3mm (⅛")
Stitch Width: M or ¼" (6mm)
Cutting Blade: OFF
Serger Thread: Standard
Attachment: Bias binder accessory
Foot: Standard

6 Cut one end of the binding flush with the edge of the bath mitt, then cut the other end of the binding about 1" (25mm) longer than the bath mitt.

SERGER SETTINGS
(STEP 7)

4-Thread Overlock

Stitch Length: 3mm (⅛")

Stitch Width: M or ¼" (6mm)

Cutting Blade: ON

Serger Thread: Standard

Foot: Standard

8 Turn the mitt right side out.

7 With right sides together, serge around the remainder of the bath mitt, folding the tail of the binding around the edge of the mitt before you serge the edge.

MATERIALS LIST

* Fingertip towel (bib)
* 3" × 12" (8cm × 30cm) ribbed knit
* Coordinating serger thread

SERGER SETTINGS

4-Thread Overlock
Stitch Length: 3mm (⅛")
Stitch Width: M or ¼" (6mm)
Cutting Blade: ON
Serger Thread: Standard
Foot: Standard

SEAM ALLOWANCE

¼" (6mm)

baby bib

When my boys were babies, my favorite bib was one that pulled over their heads—no strings to tie. I could get the bib on and off with one hand while holding the baby with the other. It was a plain little bib, but I loved it for its convenience.

Today, stores have the cutest decorative fingertip towels for every season, holiday and bath decor. It's easy to transform one into the favorite bib of any mom.

Basic Project Instructions

1 Create a template by drawing a circle with a 5" (13cm) radius on a piece of paper. Add quarter placement marks on the circle. Cut out the template and position it on the finger tip towel (see photo for positioning). Transfer the circle and the quarter placement marks. Cut out the neck opening.

2 With right sides together, serge the 3" (8cm) ends of the ribbed knit together. Add quarter placement marks approximately every 2⅞" (7cm), beginning at the seam.

Fold the ribbed knit in half lengthwise and press flat.

3 Align the quarter placement marks on the neck opening and ribbed knit piece and pin the ribbed knit to the fingertip towel.

4 Stretching the ribbed knit as you go, serge the knit to the fingertip towel. Take care to remove the pins as you serge.

5 Press the seam toward the towel and away from the ribbed knit. Your bib is complete.

MATERIALS LIST

* Fingertip towel (bib)
* 1¼ yard (1.1m) length of bias strip (width to fit the serger bias binding accessory)
* Coordinating serger thread
* Spray starch
* Bias binding accessory

SERGER SETTINGS

Settings vary in Step 3.

Wide Cover Stitch
Stitch Length: 3mm (⅛")
Stitch Width: M or ¼" (6mm)
Cutting Blade: OFF
Serger Thread: Standard
Foot: Standard

SEAM ALLOWANCE

¼" (6mm)

stepped-up
baby bib

Some parents prefer bibs that tie, especially since pulling a bib over your child's head can mess up his or her hair. Since I had little boys, this wasn't much of an issue; however, out of consideration for all the little girls with lovely locks, I've included a project for a bib that ties.

This bib also gives you the opportunity to use a cover stitch as a hem--an opportunity to strengthen your serger skills. Enjoy your final challenge!

Stepped-Up Project Instructions

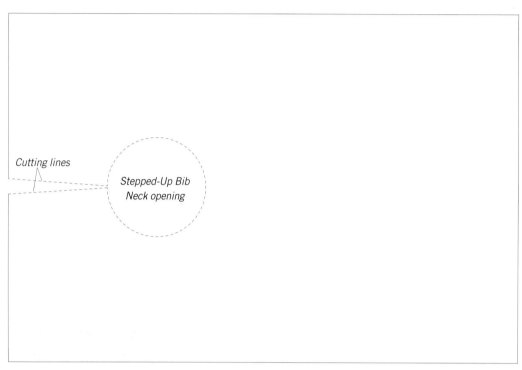

Cutting lines

*Stepped-Up Bib
Neck opening*

**Diagram of Cutting Lines and Neck Opening on
Fingertip Towel**

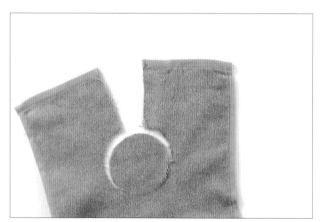

1 Create a template by drawing a circle with a 5"
(13cm) radius on a piece of paper and cut out.
Following the diagram above, transfer the circle opening
to the fingertip towel and mark the neck cutting lines.
Cut out the complete neck opening.

2 Using the wide cover stitch, hem the cut ends of
the towel by stitching the topside of the pressed
area, guiding the cut edge between the needles.

SERGER SETTINGS
(STEP 3)

Chain Stitch

Stitch Length: 3mm (⅛")

Stitch Width: M or ¼" (6mm)

Cutting Blade: OFF

Serger Thread: Standard

Foot: Standard

Attachment: Bias binding accessory

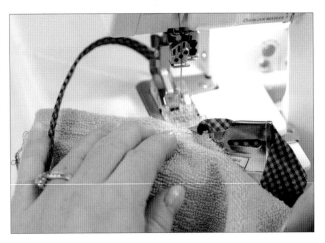

4 Stitch a 12" (30cm) tail before inserting the neck of the bib into the binding foot. Stitch a second 12" (30cm) tail after binding the neck of the bib.

5 Cut any excess binding from the tails (i.e., the ties) of the bib and apply a seam sealant on the cut ends.

3 Starch the bias strip and insert it into the bias binding accessory.

6 Allow the seam sealant to dry. Tie the bow and your bib is complete.

Index

Index

More Fast, Fun and Easy Stitching

Sew It In Minutes
24 Projects to Fit Your Style and Schedule
by Chris Malone

Discover how to create each of the 24 projects in this book in 60, 90, 120, 240 minutes or less. Projects include ornaments, photo frames, appliquéd bib and more. *Paperback, 128 pages, #Z0133. ISBN-10: 0-89689-358-8; ISBN-13: 978-0-89689-358-0*

Sew Easy as Pie
by Chris Malone

This tasty collection of 15 "easy-as-pie" projects for the kitchen is complemented by 8 scrumptious pie recipes that can be baking while projects are stitched. Projects include place mats, napkins, hot pads, curtains and more. *Paperback, 144 pages, #Z0976. ISBN-10: 0-89689-550-5; ISBN-13: 978-0-89689-550-8*

Raggedy Reverse Appliqué
10+ Fast, Fun and Forgiving Quilt Projects
by Kim Deneault

Discover a stress-free new appliqué technique through detailed instructions and 175 color photos and illustrations in this book. In addition, you'll find 12+ designs for small, quick projects, plus more complex projects, featured on a pattern insert. *Paperback, 128 pages, #Z0765. ISBN-10: 0-89689-494-0; ISBN-13: 978-0-89689-494-5*

Sip 'n Sew
20+ Home-Sewn Gifts and Refreshing Drinks
by Diane Dhein

Stitch delightful gifts for family and friends and serve up delicious drinks sure to tempt the taste buds! Features 24 projects for the home along with 20 delightful drink recipes, all quick and easy to make. *Paperback, 160 pages, #Z0981. ISBN-10: 0-89689-552-1; ISBN-13: 978-0-89689-552-2*

90-Minute Fabric Fun
30 Projects You Can Finish in an Afternoon
by Terrie Kralik

Create 30 beautiful projects for the home or to give as gifts, including fabric boxes and bowls using techniques explained and demonstrated in 200 detailed color photos. *Paperback, 144 pages, #Z0102. ISBN-10: 0-89689-377-4; ISBN-13: 978-0-89689-377-1*

These books and other fine Krause Publications titles are available at your local craft retailer or bookstore or from online suppliers.

Discover imagination, innovation and inspiration at **www.mycraftivity.com**. Connect. Create. Explore.